Praise for
Punch Doubt in the Face: How to Upskill, Change Careers, and Beat the Robots

Early on in Punch Doubt in the Face: How to upskill, change careers, and beat the robots, *Nicolle admits that professional reinvention is an act of rebellion. This book provides a helping, but not coddling, hand to those who want to make a change. Its grasp on reality, empowering tone, and dash of humor combine to create an accessible and supportive guide to the rebellion that is changing your professional trajectory.*

—Amma Marfo
Consultant and Founder, The Defectors

Punch Doubt in the Face *is the salted caramel of career management books. It's readily available, delicious, and mandatory reading. While it paints a candid picture of current and future work, this is no tome of gloom and doom. The overarching call to mine your curiosity to become a more agile worker is inspiring and actionable. I felt like she read my diary and used it to slay my dragons.*

—Allegra M. Sinclair
Founder and Chief Encouragement Officer,
Your Giant Within Coaching

Nicolle Merrill's new book, Punch Doubt in the Face, *sweeps away the confusion and last tendrils of 20th-century work hegemony, and ushers the reader into the new world of grabbing ownership of their professional life. Each chapter is written authentically with research-backed guidelines to propel current professionals to create career changes that resonate with the current and future business trends, along with specific options on how to keep learning. It is a life map that reminds each of us to, "Follow Your Curiosity." I will definitely be using this as required reading for all our incoming students and alumni.*

—Elizabeth Moon
Chief Diversity Officer
Associate Director, Career Development
University of California, Davis—Graduate School of Management

Powerful and playful, this book encourages us to both laugh and learn—exploring ways to evolve our careers and pursue fulfilling life paths.

—Joan Palmiter Bajorek
Founder of Women in Voice

At last! A book about how to prepare practically for the Future of Work we all keep hearing about. Nicolle, a former Yale career coach, gives really excellent advice and guidance about how to navigate the Fourth Industrial Revolution. I read a lot of career books, and this book is so timely, as we not only need to think about how we reinvent ourselves as the world changes, but also we actually need to do *something! It is time for action and Nicolle shows us how.*

—Jane Barrett
Co-founder of The Career Farm and
co-author of *Taking Charge of Your Career*

Punch Doubt in the Face *cleverly combines trend data, story, and practical steps to help career-changers embrace the future of work and thrive in the uncertainty. If you're struggling with a mediocre career and are looking for some novel insight, this book is a must-read.*

—Marie Zimenoff
CEO, Career Thought Leaders Consortium
and Resume Writing Academy

Rarely do we see such a witty, honest, candid look at the ups and downs of navigating today's complex job market and "career" journey. I've never been one for chess, but with the right attitude and an understanding of the true state of play, Nicolle makes it clear we can all take charge of the board, play to our strengths, develop new ones, and thrive in the workplace of the future...starting NOW.

—Mhorag Doig
Founder of Harbour84, a platform to connect today's agile
workers with workspaces to help them thrive

Nicolle Merrill approaches the future of career changes with just the right amount of humor, helpful statistics, and relatable experience. She's created a thorough and enjoyable guide that shows us how we each can take control of our careers, our skills, and our happiness.

—Paloma Medina
Founder, 11:11 Supply

This book is a down-to-earth, humorous, and informative look at the future of careers in the Fourth Industrial Revolution. It's a must-read for anyone in the workforce right now (even if you aren't currently job seeking) in order to understand how to navigate the future of technology and how to stay fresh in your career.

—**Mary Blalock**
Career Coach

As a career-changer and a serial pivoter, Punch Doubt in the Face *is a refreshing reminder that we are not losers, there is nothing wrong with us, and being adaptive is actually good. For those seeking a guide as you explore peeling back the next layer of your professional life, this book is a must-have how-to guide served up with humor and punchy anecdotes that are illustrative and very real.*

—**Amy Jermain**
Principal Strategist, Plumbline CoLAB

PUNCH DOUBT IN THE FACE

HOW TO UPSKILL, CHANGE CAREERS, AND BEAT THE ROBOTS

PUNCH DOUBT IN THE FACE

HOW TO UPSKILL, CHANGE CAREERS, AND BEAT THE ROBOTS

NICOLLE MERRILL

PUBLISH
YOUR
PURPOSE°
PRESS

Publish Your Purpose Press
141 Weston Street, #155
Hartford, CT, 06141

PUBLISH
YOUR
PURPOSE
PRESS

The opinions expressed by the Author are not necessarily those held by Publish Your Purpose Press.

Ordering Information: Quantity sales and special discounts are available on quantity purchases by corporations, associations, and others. For details, contact the publisher at orders@publishyourpurposepress.com.

Edited by: Sarina Sandstrom
Cover design by: Faaizah Ali
Typeset by: Medlar Publishing Solutions Pvt Ltd., India

Printed in the United States of America.
ISBN: 978-1-946384-86-7 (paperback)
ISBN: 978-1-946384-87-4 (hardcover)
ISBN: 978-1-946384-88-1 (ebook)

Library of Congress Control Number: 2019911626

First edition, October 2019.

The information contained within this book is strictly for informational purposes. The material may include information, products, or services by third parties. As such, the Author and Publisher do not assume responsibility or liability for any third-party material or opinions. The publisher is not responsible for websites (or their content) that are not owned by the publisher. Readers are advised to do their own due diligence when it comes to making decisions.

Publish Your Purpose Press works with authors, and aspiring authors, who have a story to tell and a brand to build. Do you have a book idea you would like us to consider publishing? Please visit PublishYourPurposePress.com for more information.

Table of Contents

PART THREE

———

How to Be an Agile Career-Changer

PART FOUR

———

Living Your Fabulously New Professional Life

Introduction:
Wrangling the Career Chaos

When do our careers officially begin? When do they officially end?

Traditional career advice tells us that our careers begin at graduation and end with a retirement party. We've been raised to think that all we need to do is go to college, pick the right major, work hard for a company, and the dollars and upward success will flow.

In the new world of work, that's an outdated fantasy. If you're stuck in a mediocre job, laid off despite working hard, or struggling to pay student loans while following your passion, you know that you don't just hop on a professional people mover and arrive at career success. Careers are messy things, full of twists, dips, and do-overs. Nothing is guaranteed.

The questions posed above aren't terribly helpful for career-changers. So, let's reframe the question. How do you know when your career is a disaster?

Answering this question gets you closer to career success. When you're struggling in your career, it's the perfect opportunity to take stock of things. It's a chance to question your job, evaluate your employer, and reflect on your needs. It also gives you permission to change and create a new path out of the mess.

Our new world of work is full of change, including career changes. Change is a new constant in our careers—new technology, new business models, new jobs. Employer expectations about what makes a good employee have changed. The most in-demand employees are agile workers, those who can adapt to new business models, work across disciplines, and learn new skills on the fly.

Our world of work has changed but the career advice you've been given since you were a kid has not. We're still following traditional career advice from a time when company plaques and parking spots were considered top company perks. You've been told that if you worked hard, your employer would reward you with raises and promotions. You've been taught to stay put in a company so you don't hurt your résumé. You weren't taught to change.

Traditional career advice is a recipe for disaster and depression in our new world of work. Our career paths do not map to our parents' careers. Employer loyalty is over. The career ladder is dead. Job-hopping is the new normal. We're all just trying to keep up.

We also face a new career reality: employers are working to replace you with robots in the form of automated platforms. Traditional career advice hasn't prepared you for these robots. A good résumé won't save you from them either.

You might have already noticed that the rules of career success have changed. Maybe you noticed when you or a family member was laid off, despite hard work and dedication. Maybe you thought things were different when you realized your passion doesn't pay your student loans. Maybe you noticed when you tried to stick to one passion but job-hopped around to explore all your other passions. Maybe the headlines about robots taking our jobs made you realize your college degree isn't enough to keep you employed in the future.

Your career path is no longer a career ladder. It's more like a Choose Your Own Adventure book. It's filled with choices and unknown paths. You're expected to explore and choose a variety of career paths throughout your life. There are surprises and adventures—all without guarantees. If you make a mistake, you can start over. You are always allowed to change your mind.

This book is designed for career-changers like you who want to wrangle the career chaos so that it works for you, not against you. There's never been a better time to change careers. You have more access to learning experiences and people than previous generations. Companies are evolving and creating new types of work for agile, curious workers like you.

All you need is a bit of direction, a dose of motivation, and time to make a career change happen.

You are not alone

If you feel that your career path has become something of a train wreck, you're not alone. Previous generations have raised us to be good, loyal employees, despite the fact that organizations are not benevolent. Today's employers are blowing up traditional career paths and expect you to keep up. If not, they'll replace you. Our employers have created this new chaos. Your goal as a career-changer is to wrangle it.

The good news is that the future of work isn't set in stone. All of us have a role in shaping the future. You have the potential to redefine your career and succeed during ambiguous times. Learning how to change your career and keep up with the chaos is an investment in your professional self. It ensures you stay relevant in the career chaos ahead.

Even better news: there's never been a better time to reshape your professional goals. You have access to opportunities to learn new skills, including ones that don't bury you in student loan debt. Traditional career paths inside organizations that follow the outdated career model are rare. Instead, companies are creating new jobs for interdisciplinary workers and creative people who don't fit traditional molds. You can find opportunities inside this chaos, shape new careers paths, and enjoy your work.

I'm on a mission to help people experiment with their careers. I want you to get unstuck and break free from your mediocre job to find a career that motivates you. Most importantly, I want you to become an agile worker who can move seamlessly between careers and navigate our new world of work.

The lifelong career is dead and we should celebrate it. We now have the freedom to explore different types of work and organizations that previous generations didn't have. We can experiment with our work and, if it doesn't work out, we can change.

This book won't help you figure out what you want to do for the rest of your life because forever careers are gone. Instead, I aim to get you out of your mediocre job and onto a new career path that fits your needs and supports your lifestyle. I will give you tools and exercises to help you get unstuck and build momentum for a career change. Better yet, the tools and framework in this book will prepare you for your next career move and every move after that.

Making a career change means making small choices that move you forward. I'm going to introduce you to you those choices throughout this book. This book isn't meant to be read straight through. It's designed to offer you action steps and get you to make choices.

So, here's your first choice:

If all of this sounds good to you, turn to page 1.

If that doesn't sound good to you, feel free to give this book a shove right off the shelf. Just be kind and put it back on the shelf so the bookstore employee doesn't have to do it.

PART ONE

The Career Ladder Rebellion

CHAPTER 1

Reinvent Your Professional Self

A Toast to Mediocre Jobs

Mediocre: neither good nor bad; tolerable

This book is for anyone who's stuck in a mediocre job. It's designed to take you step by step through the process of changing your career. You'll learn how to figure out what you want to do, how to build new skills, and how to thrive in a new world of work with ambiguous career paths. At the end of this, you'll have a road map to a better career.

But before I can show you any of that, I needed to make space for mediocre jobs. Mediocre jobs come in all shapes and sizes. They are the jobs where you aren't valued, you feel stagnant, or you lack impact. If the thought of showing up for another day of work makes you want to hide in bed, you're definitely in a mediocre job.

In the summer of 2008, I worked in a mediocre job. I had just graduated into an economy that was settling into the financial crash. Dream jobs seemed nonexistent. My dream job at the time—a university study abroad advisor—was nowhere to be found. Everyone I knew was working a mediocre job. Jobs that gave us little joy but paid the bills and not much else. I had rent, food, and student loans to pay. So, I found a job as a temporary administrative assistant for a regional insurance company.

Now there's nothing mediocre about an administrative assistant job. Administrative assistants are the power brokers of an organization. They decide who gets access to the decision-makers. They are resourceful, influential people who work behind the scenes to keep management afloat.

The problem was that I was a temporary worker hired to fill in for someone on maternity leave. Temporary work is always mediocre. I was paid less than everyone else for the same work. My temporary status put me at the bottom of a pecking order. I had zero power, which meant I was assigned the tasks that other administrative assistants didn't want.

One of those tasks was cleaning the boardroom at the end of the day. Each day at 4:45 p.m., I went to the 12th floor. While taking in the sweeping views of Portland, Oregon, I wiped down a day's worth of mayo smudges and food bits on the 14-person conference table. I realigned the table mats just so, creating an inviting space for our leadership to rest their delicate hands. I cleared the piles of leftover food overflowing in the trash and sprayed the rooms to mask the smell of sweaty bodies and feet. And every day I fought the urge to draw a big cartoon penis on the giant Post-It Super Sticky Easel Pad.

At 4:55 p.m., when nobody was around and the day's meetings had ended, I would stand in front of that 3×2-foot pad of paper perched on an easel. I would imagine how big I'd draw it. I planned to draw it on the second page so that everyone would discover it in the middle of a meeting. I would imagine the room full of executives droning on about KPIs. Some unlucky scribe would write the notes on the giant pad. When they used up the first page in a fit of brainstorming, they'd turn the page and see the offensive penis staring back at them. I debated whether or not to include googly eyes.

I'd imagine them finding it. The meeting would come to a halt amid stifled giggles and pretend shock. The rumors would begin the minute the meeting ended. There would be talk of an investigation. A giant game of whodunnit and constant gossip would entertain me for weeks.

In mediocre jobs with no future promise, we do what gets us by. Plotting to draw a giant penis on the corporate boardroom got me by.

[Spoiler alert: I never drew the penis. I talked a big game. I told my roommates every day that I'd do it. But I didn't.]

Instead, I realized I needed to apply my creativity in a way that didn't put me at risk of losing my mediocre job. I was bored but I still had bills to pay. Tired of being bored, I took a step forward.

I set up a Twitter account and started sharing articles on Twitter about ideas that interested me. Twitter was like lazy blogging. I could share information and look like an expert, all without having to write a 500-word blog post. It gave me an outlet from my mediocre job, keeping me engaged with professional subjects that interested me. I contributed to online discussions in the industry that interested me and kept up with trends.

It paid off. A CEO at an international education tech startup saw my tweets and thought I had good ideas. We had a conversation about my interests and skills. Eventually, I jumped from working as a temporary administrative assistant to working with university clients at a London-based startup. The job fueled my intellectual interests, included better pay, and gave me more responsibility than scheduling management all day. The experience also taught me that you never know where an opportunity might pop up.

In tales of career success, you rarely hear about the mediocre jobs. Yet mediocre jobs are gifts to career-changers. They let us know when it's time to change it up.

Mediocre jobs ask us to reflect and pay attention. They force us to check in with our professional selves and ask the hard questions:

- Is this really what you want?
- Why are you staying in a job that's not good for you?
- What's stopping you from change?

Reflection is key for career-changers. Change is hard. Ignoring the reasons why we need to change careers is much easier. The act of reflection forces us to confront the issues. When we confront them, we open ourselves up to solutions. Taking a step toward a new career doesn't mean having it all figured out. Sometimes the first step is simply identifying why you're stuck.

We must get more comfortable talking about our mediocre jobs. The more we talk about the work we want and imagine the path to better possibilities, the more we normalize career changes. We have been raised under a cult of employer loyalty. We've been socialized to be grateful for any job an employer deems us worthy of. The result is that many people feel guilt and failure when it comes time to change from an unsatisfying career path. They blame themselves for ending up in a mediocre place. We rarely blame employers for offering up such unfulfilling work.

A career change is an act of rebellion. It's a challenge to anyone who told us we have to choose one path. It's an act that defies a rigid career ladder model of work, giving us more freedom and flexibility to define a professional life that matches our needs. Career changes offer a do-over and a chance to redefine priorities.

There's no shame in seeking a different career path, one that fits your life better, pays better, and engages you. It's also a smart move, especially since we're heading into a new world of work that will require you to change careers multiple times in your life to keep your skills relevant in the workplace.

So, let's raise our glass and toast to all the mediocre jobs out there. May we find them, use them to light fires under our asses, and then move on better opportunities, with zero fucks given.

With Love, From A Pro Career-Changer

I'm a career hustler with a ridiculous amount of career changes and jobs under my belt. I've job-hopped more than 20 times, creating a patchwork career that has crossed continents. Since I was 14, I've worked as a lifeguard at a Vegas casino, a private jet travel writer, a temporary administrative assistant, a global program manager in Thailand, a retail sales clerk, a conversation designer for a chatbot, an adventure travel sales person in New Zealand, a staffing recruiter, a warehouse stocker on the overnight shift, and a furniture mover, among other jobs. I've changed careers three times in the past 10 years to ensure my skills stay relevant. As I write this book, I am in the middle of another career change, this time focusing on the ethical design of algorithms. Professional reinvention is my specialty. Skill collecting is my obsession.

I'm also a professional career coach who hustled my way into a job at Yale. In 2014, I landed a job as the Associate Director of Career Services at Yale School of Management. For two years, I coached MBA students and global executives through their career transitions. I listened to the dreams, insecurities, and frustrations of hundreds of career-changers. I helped global executives get unstuck and taught them how to build digital communication skills. I listened to recruiters from around the world talk about the challenges they faced finding the right people in a changing world of work. I taught people how to hustle.

I am not a typical Ivy League girl, I just played one for two years. I'm a first-generation college student who started at community college, transferred to a state school, and graduated with a mountain of student loan debt. Later, I got a full scholarship to a graduate school in northern Denmark. So, when I got the job at Yale School of Management, I felt like I'd stepped into another world. In truth, I stepped into another class, one that came with name brands, connections, and tidy professional boxes.

I soon learned, however, that despite the class differences, career-changers across cultures and classes share similar worries. I learned that everyone experiences doubt and fear about their career. Some are just really good at hiding it. I discovered that all career-changers are balancing expectations from family and friends. I coached many career-changers through identity crises, people who thought they'd become one thing and decided they wanted another. I also saw beautiful results and wins. Career changes come with a lot of frustration but they nearly all result in joy.

I also learned that outside of professional degree programs like MBAs, few of us are taught how to change careers. MBA students are given space to explore new career options. They're taught how to build professional communication skills and translate their learning experiences into qualifications. They're taught how to present themselves and evaluate their options.

Nobody ever taught me that. Chances are, you haven't learned how to do that either.

Comfort is the opposite of career progression

During my work at Yale, I spoke with recruiters and hiring managers all over the world, including at Google, Amazon, Alibaba, IDEO, and more. I also spoke with founders at startups who were experimenting with new ways of work. I learned how new and emerging business models are changing the type of employee that employers seek. Employers are all seeking interdisciplinary unicorns: people who can solve complex problems, communicate well, make sense of data, contribute creative ideas to their department, translate feedback into action, and work across departments with ease. Not all MBA students were prepared to become this new type of employee. Listening to employers question whether or not elite graduate students had the right skills made me wonder how my own skills were holding up.

I loved my work and coworkers at Yale. My job came with a brand name, prestige, and more money than I'd ever made. I was grateful for the opportunity and comfortable in my career. I probably could have sailed along in that role for as long as I liked.

But those conversations with employers challenged me to reflect on my own future. I started paying attention to how technology and business practices are reshaping organizations and the nature of work. When I examined my department and the industry, I saw no options to learn the cutting-edge skills that employers seek. My employer was resistant to change. Management was inflexible. I felt stuck.

I realized that if I stayed on my comfortable career path in higher education, I risked becoming irrelevant in the future of work. I also realized that career coaches like me were recycling outdated career advice that didn't prepare people for the new realities of the workplace.

It seemed crazy to leave such a good job, but I didn't want to get left behind. After all, you don't learn new skills from inside the comfort zone. So, I did what was necessary. I took a step forward toward change by jumping off of my career path in higher education. A year and a half later, I started on a new career path as a conversation designer for a chatbot working for an artificial intelligence startup. Now I'm immersed in a world of data, technology, and artificial intelligence. I'm tapping into skills that I've honed over the course of several careers while building new skills. This new career path challenges me and keeps my skills sharp.

In this book, I'm wrangling all of the experience above to help you change careers and remain relevant in a fast-changing world of work. I'm a job-hopper who has hustled my way into different organizations, across borders, and between industries for the majority of my career. I'm also a former Ivy League career coach with years of experience helping career-changers at all stages of their professional lives. I drop F-bombs, procrastinate hard, and get too loud in open workspaces. But that's the funny thing about professional lives: we can be many imperfect things at once and still make it work. Professional perfection is overrated.

I'm going to take you on a wild ride of career advice that starts in the past, travels to the future, takes a dip into the imaginary, and brings you back to the present, all in an effort to get you on the path to a better professional life. So, stick with me.

An Act of Professional Reinvention

Career changes are an act of professional reinvention. We grew up learning that work is our identity. We've been taught to pick our path, get into a company, and move up. The path you took and the title you earned became your identity. Deviating from that path was frowned upon. I was expected to have a single career path from the moment I declared my major. As a French literature major with massive student debt, that was never going to happen for me.

Since we've been raised with this mentality, the work of reinventing our professional selves feels like an uphill battle. From the minute you declare your intent to change, people ask you to define yourself. *What do you want to be? What do you do?* These are terribly unhelpful questions. They force us into a single path with a single identity:

I am a ____. I want to be a _____.

The problem with this is that you aren't just a _____. You are a _____ and a ____ and ____ who _____ and _____. Our professional lives are a game of Mad Libs (and full of run-on sentences). We all bring diverse interests and goals to our professional lives. I am a person who loves to talk to large groups of people and get paid for it. Someone who gets a crazy high from audience laughter, agitates to change the status quo, and cheers on the underdogs. Our professional interests and personalities don't always fit neatly into one job title or a single lifelong path. Our professional interests and needs change over time. And that's perfectly okay.

Declaring your intent to reinvent your professional self is an act of rebellion. At the start of a career change, there are plenty of unknowns. The ambiguity of it makes people uncomfortable. It forces others to reflect on their own career choices. People respond by asking for clarity, hoping for a nice tidy package you can give them, so they won't worry so much.

Our careers are full of chaos, yet we're all pretending that they are polished, tidy things because our work is so closely tied to our identity. In American culture, the pressure to appear like you have your professional shit together is everywhere. We are bombarded with affirmations and demands to be a boss, create our brand, lead boldly, and reach our goals. Behind those beautifully curated images is a mass of people riding the professional struggle bus.

I know this because career coaches know people's professional secrets. As a professional career coach, I've listened to hundreds of people tell me their professional fears and insecurities. From global executives who worried about their inability to write good emails to students from elite universities who needed to escape the brutal grind of management consulting to entrepreneurs who wanted to leave their startups, I have listened to professionals struggle with their personal career chaos.

It's not just the elite who are trying to hide their professional chaos. I've listened to hundreds of strangers and friends as they navigated career chaos. After all, career coaches aren't constrained to giving advice between the hours of 9 a.m. and 5 p.m. My particular specialty is drunk career coaching. I have a habit of career coaching strangers at bars. The minute a stranger tells me they hate their job, I'm in career coach mode, beer in hand. The stranger gets a sympathetic ear and some sloppy but sound advice. I get a free beer or three, depending on how long it takes to hear their professional struggle story. I listen to their stories, empathize with their situation, and wait for their secrets to surface, aided, of course, by booze.

In those conversations, I listen to the challenges people feel when it comes time to change careers. People share stories of doubt, wondering if they are too old, too young, too stuck, too dumb, too unsure to make a change. I hear stories of insecurity brought on by abusive bosses and poor company culture. I listen to people worry about their obligation to their employers, despite the fact that our employers lack an obligation to their workers. I hear about family pressures, money troubles, and lack of access to new educational opportunities. I hear the doubt.

I also hear brilliant stories. I listen to people share their ideas, hopes, dreams, loves, and more than one declaration that they're going to make the change starting tomorrow. Of course, I rarely learn how they turn out, but I love the enthusiasm. Sometimes all people need is a cheerleader and someone to point them in the right direction.

Despite all the struggles, none of these people are hopeless. Getting stuck in your career isn't a hopeless place. It's a starting place. The fact that you're stuck isn't all your fault. After all, you haven't been taught how to change careers. Because we haven't learned, we're forced to stumble around trying to figure it out. Some of us get lucky. Others stay stuck for a while until we can't take it anymore. Others get laid off and scramble to make a change.

I am eternally grateful for all who have trusted me to listen to their professional secrets. All of the stories and qualitative data allow me to tell you, with confidence and love, that you are not alone in your career chaos. Everyone thinks everyone else has it together. Nobody does. Reinventing your professional self is hard in a culture that asks for perfection and certainty in all aspects of our professional lives.

There's never been a better time to reinvent your professional self. You are surrounded by learning opportunities to build new skills and explore new fields. New technology makes it easy to find, follow, and engage with professionals who inspire us. You have the flexibility to experiment with options, try new career paths, and learn from what doesn't fit.

The formula for professional reinvention

A career change takes a lot more than finding jobs online and writing résumés. In fact, you have to tap into a whole set of skills to make a career change. You use project management, communication, knowledge management, and time management skills. It's a lot of managing yourself. Since the self-help industry is valued at nearly $10 billion, I'd say we're collectively not very good at self-management. So, cut yourself some slack for being on the struggle circuit. It's not easy.

A career change is different from simply changing jobs. It's not just changing up a bad boss or switching to a new environment. A career change is a shift into a new function and field with the intent to improve your professional life.

How you define improvement is up to you. For some, it's an improvement in salary or work-life balance. For others, it's a chance to improve your skills or work for a company that has a positive impact on society. No matter your reason for seeking improvement, a career jump is a strategic move.

The formula for a career change is simple:

**Identify professional interests + Get new skills +
Learn new domain knowledge = New career**

Your professional interests are the types of work and organizations that interest you. Skills are your ability to do the tasks that a job requires. Domain knowledge is the vocabulary and expertise required to understand how a job fits into an organization. The path to a career change is also simple:

**Identify your next career move → Analyze your skill and
experience gaps → Learn the skills and knowledge you need
to make the jump → Get the job**

The path is simple, but the process is complicated by time, money, and our own brains. The time it takes to accomplish that is different for everyone.

Traditionally, if a person wanted to change careers, they would go back to school. If you chose an MBA as the path to a new career, you'd spend on average of $80,000 for a two-year program. You'd take off two years from work, which would cost you two years' worth of salary. Since our new work reality is a future filled with multiple career changes, it's not sustainable to go back to school every five years. Unless you've got a trust fund or really love student loans, you must learn how to change careers without relying on traditional degree programs each time.

Thankfully, we live in a time where access to information is unparalleled. New educational models like online programs and coding bootcamps have evolved to help career-changers like you. Community colleges are creating innovative educational programs in partnership with local employers. Apprenticeships are thriving, creating sustainable, robot-proof jobs in the trades. Some forward-thinking employers are starting to offer education benefits again and invest in training opportunities.

Our access to DIY learning is also unprecedented. According to the Pew Research Center, 51 percent of YouTube users are looking at how-to videos, with over 30 percent of users looking for career-related information. Many of us engage in self-directed learning on a regular basis through podcasts, online videos, and social communities. These micro-learning experiences are all pieces of the career change puzzle. Depending on your career path, you can use these tools to help you make a career change.

Career Changes Are the New Normal

Listening to little kids tell us what they want to be when they grow up is cute. They're full of giggles and wonder. We ask them, "What will you be when you grow up?" The kids delight us with their answers, screaming things like, "A singer! An astronaut! A doctor!"

Kids are free to dream up what they'd like to be well throughout their childhood. Sometime in high school they start experimenting with actual work. Babysitting, yard work, coding websites, becoming social media influencers. When those kids slide into early adulthood, experienced adults change the question to: "What will you do with that?" *That* could be a job that pays the bills, a college major with undefined career paths, or an adventurous travel experience outside of the traditional career path.

The question implies that at some point you'll settle on a professional calling and stick with it. And if you haven't found it yet, you should be working toward it. If you go to college, you're given assessments to help you understand your personality. The idea is that you'll discover what to be for the rest of your life. In college you must pick a major, a subject that is supposed to be your jumping off point into a lifelong career. We are not given space to explore or change.

Society expects us to settle on a career choice early in our adulthood. Once we've decided, we're supposed to chase that thing up a career ladder, always heading upward, toward a vague idea of success. This expectation is baked into the definition of the word career: "an occupation undertaken for a significant period of a person's life and with opportunities for progress."[1]

The problem is that careers are no longer lifelong commitments. Even if we all collectively decided to stay put in our careers, only 19 percent of companies now have traditional career pathways.[2] That means employers don't even have the opportunities in place to provide lifetime career paths for their employees. So, why are we pretending we're going to pursue one career path for a lifetime?

Death to the career ladder

Career ladder is a metaphor for job promotion. In business and human resources management, the career ladder typically describes the progression from entry-level positions to higher levels of pay, skill, responsibility, or authority. This metaphor is spatially oriented, and frequently used to denote upward mobility within a stratified promotion model. Because

---

[1] *Oxford Dictionaries*, "Career."
[2] Deloitte Insights, "Changing Nature of Careers."

*the career ladder does not provide for lateral movement, it is assumed to
be a singular track with the greatest benefits at the top.* —*Wikipedia*[3]

Reading that definition makes it obvious that career ladders
are terribly outdated. The career ladder model envisions a time
of career stability, one that doesn't include mass layoffs. It also
doesn't account for the new ways in which people work. These
days our careers are a mix of full-time and part-time jobs, gig
work, side hustles, entrepreneurship, freelance opportunities, and
flex work. In 2018, 36 percent of Americans worked as freelanc-
ers. A survey by Freelancing in America found that "50.9 percent
of the US population will be freelancing in 10 years if a current
uptick in freelancing continues at its current pace."[4] Freelancing
doesn't even have a rung on the career ladder.

The career ladder also fails to make room for lateral movements. Yet these movements serve an important purpose in our
careers. Lateral movements expose us to new skills, expand
our network, and revitalize us when we're feeling stagnant or
burned out.

Worse, the career ladder model is designed for only half the
population. It's rooted in that old-school mentality where women
did the caregiving and men climbed their company ladder to success. Parenting and caregiving are also missing from the career
ladder. Thanks to the career ladder mentality, parents and caregivers, who are mostly women, are penalized when they step off
the ladder. Caregivers who need to take time out of the workforce
are considered less employable because they've stepped off the
career ladder. This mentality is garbage, especially when plenty

---

[3]Wikipedia, "Career ladder."
[4]Forbes, "Workforce."

of parents engage in side work, freelance, and volunteer on top of raising the future generation—an endless responsibility that isn't even considered work.

But what's particularly terrible about the career ladder model is that it has forced many into bad career decisions. People take jobs they don't want because, well, it's the next step on the ladder. Coworkers turn into bad managers because management is always the next step. Middle managers compete for increasingly smaller opportunities at the top because it's the next step on the ladder. We're rarely taught about an option outside of the career ladder: the individual contributor.

Individual contributors are experts inside an organization who contribute to multiple teams. They take on special projects, use a variety of skills, and get shit done. They're also paid well for it. There is no rung on the career ladder for individual contributors.

The career ladder reinforces the idea that the best benefits are always at the top, always out of reach. But that's not true either. There are companies paying good, livable salaries for highly skilled workers who aren't at the top.

It's hard to defy the career ladder. The concept is ingrained in our educational system. It's reinforced in business culture with a never-ending focus on leadership as the sole definer of career success. We are told we must climb and climb and climb some more until we're on top and leading the pack. Success is an extreme sport in American culture. That approach works for some. But not for most.

Sometimes it's not in our best interest to move up. Other times we need to move to the side. And still other times we need to pause.

Thankfully, we're living in a time when the old career rules no longer apply. As a career-changer, you don't need to move up.

You also don't need to move down. You can move diagonally. The direction is irrelevant. The point is to just move.

So, let's all take a moment to mentally burn down the career ladder and shout good riddance. We don't need it anymore.

Our careers are chess boards

Our career model needs an upgrade to reflect the new world of work. We need options that are agile and allow us to move freely and strategically.

The ideal model for careers is more like a chess game. In chess, you choose the best tool to succeed. You look beyond the next step to explore all possibilities. You could be the pawn, which moves in all directions except backward but later gains the power to be anything it wants when it reaches its opponent's side. You could be the rook, which only moves in the path of an uppercase L, basically floating over anything in its way. Or the queen, which goes any direction she damn well pleases. In your career, the goal is to stay one step ahead of your employers. That means taking a strategic approach by always looking ahead, surveying your choices, and adapting your path and tools to get to your goal.

For career-changers, the chess board model provides much more flexibility. A career change is a diagonal move. You might not keep the hot job title, but you might build valuable new skills. You might make less money in your next move, but you might gain more time with loved ones. These aren't backward moves. These are diagonal moves. With each career move you bring all the skills and experience into your next step, no matter which direction it goes.

Everything we've been taught about career planning has changed. Our careers are much more flexible than those of the previous generations. You're allowed to change your mind. You're not tied to a college major or an employer who isn't good to you. If the job you're working in isn't meeting your needs, you can and should find something better. Employers are no longer in control of our career plans. You have the freedom to customize your own.

Forever careers are over

You likely started your career with the question: "What do I want to do with the rest of my life?" It's a question that puts a lot of unnecessary pressure to pick a career path that will satisfy all our financial, intellectual, and lifestyle needs at every stage of our lives.

Imagine if we asked each other a different question about our career paths. What if we asked, "How do you want to live?" Imagine how we might answer that. We might pick a career path that fits our needs and life experiences, instead of one that doesn't work, plowing forward on a path because we committed to it 10 years ago. We might allow ourselves to change course, to be honest about what we need from our work.

Once I took a job in New Zealand selling adventure travel because I wanted to get paid while traveling in a foreign country. I quit a full-time corporate job to do it and people around me panicked. "What will you do with that?" they asked, as I veered from the traditional path. I didn't know. But I knew that I wanted to live an adventurous life outside of a cubicle. I knew how I wanted to live at that time of my life, not what I wanted to do for the rest of my life.

It's time to reframe how we think about our careers. Instead of thinking about what you want to do for the rest of your life, I want you to ask better questions: How do you want to live?

What type of work do you want to do that allows you to live the kind of life you want? What type of work brings you joy? Who do you want to surround yourself with in the workplace? What subjects and skills do you want to learn?

Every job you work is a career experience. Each time you take a job you learn new skills and connect with new people. Each role offers you the chance to figure out if the work you do is a fit for you in the context of your life. Through each new career experience, you learn what you like, what you love, and what you hate. All of these experiences offer valuable data points that help you shape a professional path. As your life changes—you add kids, travel, bills, caretaking, spouses—so should your career experiences.

The beauty of this approach is that you create your career experiences. Your career path is no longer shaped by the chase of a single job title on the next rung. Forever careers and career ladders are outdated relics of the past. Now, you customize your career, shaping it through choice and experiments.

As you start your career change, avoid putting pressure on yourself to find the right career forever. Instead, think of it as a path for the next three to five years, with periodic check-ins to see if your career choice is still working for you. Instead of thinking about what you want to do for the rest of your life, ask this: What are you so curious about that you could work on it for the next five years?

A career of professional jumps

Job-hopping is the new normal. That probably made some of you uncomfortable just reading that sentence. It's been drilled into our head that job-hopping is bad. Yet more people are starting to get comfortable with the idea of job-hopping, even if they're not actively talking about it. A 2018 survey by Jobvite, a recruitment software company, found that among the 61 percent of workers who are satisfied with their current jobs, 51 percent are open to changing jobs every few years.[5] A 2016 survey by Gallup found that among millennials, "only one in two plan to be with their company one year from now, while 50% say they'd consider taking a job with a different company for a raise of 20% or less."[6] Staying at your job long term can even result in less pay. The online magazine Quartz reports that a 2016 study by ADP, a national payroll processing company, found that "the longer you stay past five years, the less growth you'll see in pay at your next employer."[7]

In conversations about job-hopping the focus is always on the negative. There's a fear that future employers will punish you for not sticking it out. This fear has kept plenty of people in bad jobs or working under bad management. But employers don't care as much about job-hopping these days. They're looking for skills and more skills. Recruiters, those on the frontline of hiring you, are part of the same job-hopping generation as you. Look at recruiters' profiles on LinkedIn and you'll see plenty of job-hopping. I just looked at an Amazon recruiter's profile. One year here. One and a half years here. Two years there.

If you have a good career path that meets your needs, work in a place that treats you well and gives you the chance to develop skills, feel free to hang out there. But if you're bored, lack

---

[5] Forbes, "Workforce."
[6] Gallup, "Millennials."
[7] Quartz, "When to switch."

opportunities to develop new skills, or work in a toxic environment, then leave. Don't be a slave to the "it'll hurt my résumé" narrative. That's old-school thinking. Companies are replaceable. You customize your own career adventure.

Career jumps are big, bold moves into new professional worlds. They bring benefits, pay raises, new skills, and fresh perspectives. A career change is a jump into better professional circumstances. Career jumps incorporate existing skills and knowledge and combine them with new skills to find the next opportunity. I use the term *career jumps* because we don't let go of our experience and skills when we change. Instead, we bring them with us. We jump into new work equipped with diverse knowledge and skills built from years of working. The result is a more resourceful, agile worker.

Workers with a collection of diverse skills and experience are more valuable to employers. When you jump into a new career, you build your agility. You become an employee with a diversified skill set. You're able to adapt and collaborate with people from different backgrounds. The agile worker is the most employable type of worker in our new world of work.

Corporate America Killed Your Career

Even in the 21st century, we're still navigating our careers using 20th-century career rules. The rules go like this: Get into a company. Work hard. Stay put. You'll be rewarded. If you've worked anywhere in the last 15 years, you know this is some old-school bullshit. Yet this fantastical narrative still dominates our workplace.

This career advice is rooted in the idea of employer loyalty. In previous generations, employees trusted their employers and employers were perceived as benevolent actors. Employers would take care of you as long as you put in the time. Workplace commitment, through physical time spent at your job and tenure at the company, was highly prized. Workers were motivated by prestige and clear pathways to advancement. The motivational perks that defined this generation were as simple as prestigious job titles, plaques for multiple years of service, and saved parking spots. Employer loyalty was top of mind.

We're living in a completely different world now. As the generation that lived through the 2008 recession, we saw that hard work and employee loyalty had no bearing on who was laid off. We saw parents lose jobs and friends struggle to get jobs. Over the past 15 years, companies have continuously laid off employees, loyalty be damned. Now, corporate America's use of layoffs, temporary workers, and automated tools ensure that employer loyalty is a thing of the past.

In times of record corporate profits, corporate America is still laying off employees. In 2018, ProPublica, an investigative reporting organization, published a report called "Cutting Old Heads at IBM."[8] Their investigation found that IBM, "targeted people for layoffs and firings with techniques that tilted against older workers, even when the company rated them high performers. In some instances, the money saved from the departures went toward hiring young replacements." This is a company that had an annual revenue of over $75 billion. This isn't just people who were on the cusp of retiring. IBM targeted around 20,000 employees who were 40 and over. Worse yet, ProPublica found that IBM told some older workers that their skills were outdated and later hired them back as contractors. Contractors cost less

---

[8]ProPublica, "IBM."

for companies since they don't pay them benefits. Then there are companies like Hewlett Packard. They laid off 34,000 people in 2018 and used the term *pruning* to describe it. You prune bushes, not people, but don't tell that to HP's PR team.

Companies also rely more on temporary workers—usually independent contractors—instead of hiring full- time employees. In October 2018, Google officially had more contract workers than direct employees. That's expected to continue. One study found that 60 percent of the workforce will be independent contractors or will have worked independently by 2027. For companies, independent contractors are ideal employees. They're cheaper. They aren't offered benefits. Most don't get vacation days or sick leave.

Companies increasingly see no need to invest in you, the worker. Instead, they're actively looking for ways to replace you. In early 2019, the *New York Times* provided a warning about how giddy executives seemed at replacing workers with automation:

> *"They are racing to automate their own work forces to stay ahead of the competition, with little regard for the impact on workers. All over the world, executives are spending billions of dollars to transform their businesses into lean, digitized, highly automated operations. They crave the fat profit margins automation can deliver, and they see A.I. as a golden ticket to savings, perhaps by letting them whittle departments with thousands of workers down to just a few dozen."*[9]

---

[9]*New York Times*, "Davos Elite."

Corporate America's leadership has shown us that we are all replaceable.

Everyone is replaceable

Look around your workplace. Who do you think is replaceable? Better question: Who thinks you're replaceable? Even better question: Would you know if you were replaceable?

Here's the truth: everyone in your organization is replaceable. Your manager. Your coworker who seems like they're killing it in everything they do. The person who writes the company-wide internal emails. They're all replaceable. And so are you.

That's brutal to write. After all, we learn and perform as best we can in a job in hopes of becoming *irreplaceable*. You might be reading this and shouting at me, "BUT I'M TALENTED AND WORK HARD! I AM IRREPLACEABLE!"

I have no doubt you, dear reader, are talented and work hard, but companies already think of you as replaceable. Changes to business models mean that companies are constantly rethinking their business strategy. Executives look ahead and lay out a new strategy. Finance runs the numbers. Managers are notified of new directions and unnecessary positions. Workers who don't fit the organization's new priorities are cut. Communication departments write up the mass email praising new directions.

This happens at old-school companies as well as new ones. Take BuzzFeed, the media company built on listicles and quizzes, and later turned into a Serious Media company. BuzzFeed, like all online news and media companies, faces a constant battle to reinvent itself and tweak its business model. Journalists and creative professionals in media increasingly struggle with meager wages and job insecurity due to continuous disruption in the media industry. In the fall of 2017, BuzzFeed laid off about 100 employees. BuzzFeed President Jonah Peretti summed up the decision this way:

> *"As our strategy evolves, we need to evolve our organization, too—particularly our Business team, which was built to support direct-sold advertising but will need to bring in different, more diverse expertise to support these new lines of business. Unfortunately, this means we have to say goodbye to some talented colleagues whose work has helped us tremendously."*[10]

Here's the kicker in that statement. They admit that the people they're laying off were "talented colleagues" and even praise their work, which has helped BuzzFeed "tremendously."

Translation: We no longer need you.

Truth: We used you.

That wasn't the end of the layoffs though. In January 2018, BuzzFeed laid off another 20 percent of their staff. Here's an excerpt from the layoff letter sent to employees from Chief Revenue Officer Lee Brown:

> *"As a result, we'll be rolling out some changes to our teams and how we operate over the next couple weeks. These changes will involve bringing in new blood—we've opened more than 45 new roles across Creative, Strategic Planning, and Pricing, as well as new growth areas such as Business Development*

---

[10]Chicago Business Journal, "BuzzFeed."

and Programmatic. Please check the BuzzFeed Jobs site and share these positions across your personal networks, or apply if you're interested in new opportunities. In a handful of cases, the changes we're making will unfortunately result in some roles being eliminated. Most of those eliminated positions will be converted to new open positions in other areas of the org, and we're encouraging impacted employees to apply for new positions for which they are qualified.[11]

The PR team reframes the language of replacement by using the phrase "bringing in new blood." Those who are "impacted" are encouraged to "apply for new positions for which they are qualified." Translation: they're not even going to bother retraining the employees who are laid off.

You can't rely on hard work or charm or talent or anything else to protect you from layoffs due to change. Talent and hard work that benefit the company didn't matter at BuzzFeed. It doesn't matter at your place of work. Organizations, managers, and businesses change. Unlike your parents' employers, companies are no longer interested in ensuring every employee gets the training they need to stay relevant in their personal careers.

Flip the script

Is the company you work for replaceable? Asking the question feels a bit taboo. We are taught to commit to our place of work. Asking if the company we work for is replaceable signals our

---

[11]Vox, "BuzzFeed."

lack of commitment. Yet the question forces us to consider other questions. Does this company provide for me? Does it invest in my future? Does it value my work? If the answer to any of those questions is no, the company you work for is most definitely replaceable.

Companies expect workers to continuously improve their skills or they will be replaced. Yet, as employees, we haven't been taught to demand the same of companies. Instead of fearing our replacement, we need to examine our employers. We need to stop committing to companies that do not invest in their workforce. If a company doesn't pay you a fair wage or doesn't provide professional training to help you build new skills, they are replaceable.

Breaking the employee loyalty taboo is a challenge because companies don't want you to think of them as interchangeable organizations. Companies pretend they're your forever home. Managers still ask the interview question about where you see yourself in five years. Job seekers still answer with, "I plan to see myself here in five years." Yet a 30-minute interview isn't nearly enough time to know whether you're going to commit your professional life to a team or manager. It's like both parties agreeing on the first date that they're ready to move in together.

Acknowledging that the companies we work for are replaceable frees us to make better decisions about our careers and look for opportunities without shame. It allows us to ask more of the places we work.

I'm not the first to note this. In fact, the cofounder of LinkedIn, Reid Hoffman, called out the demise of employee loyalty, putting the blame squarely on the shoulders of companies. In the book he coauthored, *The Alliance: Managing Talent in the Networked Age*, he proposes a new career model that acknowledges the shredded employee-employer contract. He wants companies to stop pretending that employees take a job as a lifelong contract. Instead, Reid and his coauthors argue that companies should be upfront with employees that they're hired for a set amount of time. In turn, the employee is allowed to use the time to figure out if they're a fit for the company.

Reid and his coworkers gave the example of hiring an employee for four years at max. At the two-year mark, they recommend employers have a conversation about whether or not the job is still a fit for that employee. In that conversation, the employer evaluates how the employee has contributed to the company. In return, the employee is free to evaluate if the position is still a fit for them. If they both want to continue, so be it. If not, they part ways and both move on. They named this approach the Tour of Duty.

In a promotional talk for this book tour, Reid stated that job seekers and companies are lying to each other throughout the interview.

> *"They know that employers want loyalty," Hoffman says. "They know they want to hear, 'Oh, I plan on working here for the rest of my career.' But most employees recognize that career progression probably requires eventually moving to another company. But that never comes up."*[12]

In the modern workforce, everyone is replaceable. So, let's stop pretending we're loyal to companies. You are not bound to

---

[12]Vox, "LinkedIn."

your employer. You have all the power to decide when and how to leave a job. Do not feel guilty for leaving or changing directions. You can like your job, your boss, your coworkers, and even the company. And then you can leave it on your terms for something better.

Before the next section, I want you to reflect on your current employer. Is your place of work providing for you? Does it meet your needs? If not, commit to replacing it.

The future is yours

I realize at this point I've taken you through a bleak look at the reality of our workforce. But I want to shock you out of the traditional career ladder mindset. We're no longer living by old-school career rules. We have entered the age of the agile employee. The agile employee acknowledges they are replaceable but strives to be hard to replace. That difference is critical. It requires you to stay ahead of the game. At the same time, agile workers always keep an eye out for better opportunities. This shifts the balance of power. Instead of being reliant on your employer for the next steps, you call the shots.

I'm here to show you how to do this. I will show you exactly how to leave a job and change careers so you are prepared to adapt to changes in the workforce. You'll be more agile and less likely to get laid off. And even if you are laid off, you'll know how to bounce back.

Most importantly though, I want you to have less fear. There is always a risk when changing jobs or careers. That can't be eliminated. But you can eliminate the fear and insecurity that comes with changing your professional life.

Reframing companies as temporary stays helps us move forward in an ever-changing workforce. As a career-changer, it takes a lot of work. But don't worry about what employers or others will think about your loyalty. Everything has changed. You control your own career narrative now.

CHAPTER 2

The Future of Work Has Arrived

The Fourth Industrial Revolution and You

A month before I quit my job at Yale School of Management, I was at a holiday party hanging out at an exceptional cheese plate. I was deep into a manchego block when a friend of a friend walked over to me.

"Hey, I heard you're quitting your job to start your own business. You're doing something with life coaching, right?"

I was immediately taken aback, my manchego slice frozen in midair. This guy is a successful entrepreneur. I had big plans to be a successful entrepreneur too, but I hadn't even given notice at my job yet. I was in transition but didn't quite know how to talk about it. Naturally, I wanted to sound like I had my shit together. I also wanted to smack the words life coach right out of his successful mouth. Career coaches are often lumped in with life coaches. But I am most definitely *not* a life coach. I'm missing a warm and fuzzy heart to help strangers through nonwork-related issues. So, I countered his assumption:

"Actually, I'm preparing people for the Fourth Industrial Revolution."

Now it was his turn to freeze. I felt the awkward silence between us and imagined a giant WTF conversation bubble appear next to his head. A polite smile spread across his face. He leaned back and looked around, a classic conversational move that signals *I've made a huge mistake talking to this one.*

"Okay. Cool. Well, good luck in your business endeavors." And then he turned away, leaving me to my manchego. I learned two things in this conversation. #1: I needed to work on my professional story. #2: Talking about the Fourth Industrial Revolution at parties is awkward as fuck.

Career potential and peril

"I don't think anyone can do long-term career planning with any confidence. We make assumptions about the indispensability of human beings but machines are already doing things we thought only humans might be able to." —The Guardian[13]

The Fourth Industrial Revolution isn't exactly a household term. We can thank Klaus Schwab, the executive chairman and founder of the World Economic Forum (WEF), for this clumsy phrase. We can't fault him though; he's an engineer and economist, not a wordsmith. He's a serious man who's responsible for leading the World Economic Forum, a global nonprofit that brings together leaders for private-public cooperation to, "shape global, regional and industry agendas."[14]

---

[13] *Guardian* (US), "Jobs."
[14] World Economic Forum, "Mission."

The term *Fourth Industrial Revolution* emerged in 2016 from the annual World Economic Forum meeting in Davos, Switzerland. The Forum convenes an annual meeting in Davos where the world's richest people and government leaders gather to talk about the world's most pressing problems and discuss how rich people will solve them.

At the start of the 2016 WEF Davos meeting, Schwab produced the report, "The Fourth Industrial Revolution." In it, Schwab named the technological and cultural shifts that define the Fourth Industrial Revolution. In particular, he wrote of the rise of technology like artificial intelligence, big data, Internet of Things (IoT), robotics, and cloud technology, as the biggest sources of disruption. These shifts mean that businesses will need to create new business models to stay relevant. He noted that the "average lifespan of a corporation listed on the S&P 500 has dropped from around 60 to approximately 18 [years]."[15] Translation: businesses are struggling to stay relevant because new technology is destroying their business models.

New technology combined with increasing computer processing power will speed up the pace at which these technologies are adapted. Together, it creates the perfect technological innovation storm to destroy the professional lives of workers around the world. I'm simplifying a 172-page report here so your eyes don't glaze over. To say that things are changing due to new technology is an understatement. So, here's how Schwab puts it: "The changes are so profound that, from the perspective of human history, there has never been a time of greater promise or potential peril."[16]

---

[15]World Economic Forum, "Fourth Industrial Revolution."
[16]*Guardian* (US), "Fourth Industrial Revolution."

Peril. That's the word he uses to describe where we are in history in terms of technological change. Not only did Schwab carve out this period of change and name it, but he also wanted us to see that this period of disruption poses a threat to our professional livelihoods. The WEF put some numbers to the havoc that technological innovation might rain down on our professional lives. The 2016 report estimated that 7.1 million jobs might be lost between 2015 and 2020, the majority of which would be in white-collar office roles.

When the global elite says technology is about to change everything we know about the world of work, the world listens. After the report's publication, the internet lost its collective mind. The report spawned thousands of articles about the future of work featuring stories about robots taking all the jobs. Inc. com published an article called, "Robots May Take More Than 5 Million Jobs by 2020."[17] *USA Today*, wrote an article titled, "Study: Robots to nab 5.1 million jobs by 2020."[18] The *Guardian* was more creative with the ideas, writing the headline: "Terminator, Robocop and Atlas the Robot. For workers the plot is grim."[19]

Talking about robots taking jobs was all the rage in 2016. Articles like "10 high-paying jobs that will survive the robot invasion" by Workopolis Blog, and "Technology Will Replace Many Doctors, Lawyers, and Other Professionals," by *Harvard Business Review*, showed the range of ways new technology will change our career paths and plans. Predicting the future is relatively easy. There is no pressure to be right. All you need is some stats, a good story, and an audience.

---

[17] Inc., "Robots."

[18] *USA Today*, "Study."

[19] *Guardian* (US), "Terminator, Robocop and Atlas the Robot."

Two years after the WEF's original report, the numbers have shifted. In the 2018 report, "The Future of Jobs," the WEF estimated 75 million jobs will be displaced by artificial intelligence and automation. However, 133 million new jobs will be created.[20] The pace of change has increased.

While the numbers may shift over time, the takeaway is clear: technology is changing how organizations operate and the type of skills needed to succeed in the modern workplace. It's also changing how we navigate our careers.

Netflix and skill

Companies are in the midst of a digital transformation from the old economy to the new economy.

The 20th century was dominated by companies that produced physical objects: Coca-Cola, IBM, General Motors. Now, a new type of company dominates the 21st century. They're the household names that run in the background of our daily lives: Amazon, Alphabet/Google, Facebook, and Netflix.

Technology is at the heart of their business model. They specialize in digital products and services. These companies are agile and relentlessly consumer focused. They're able to launch new digital products in a short amount of time. They also attract highly skilled workers. Employees who work at these companies, and ones like them, work on challenging, complex problems. They have access to learning opportunities to build new skills that keep them relevant in the workplace.

---

[20]World Economic Forum, "Jobs."

Companies are upgrading their business models while digitizing their organizations. They are turning to digital platforms and specialized software to get work done. Increasingly, leaders collect and use large amounts of data to make critical business decisions. The transformation to digital has resulted in the need for employees with a new set of skills.

Employers want employees with digital skills. Technology and digital fluency are no longer limited to IT workers. Digital is becoming embedded into the fabric of our jobs. If you're an employee who doesn't understand data analytics, struggles to learn new software, or can't collaborate with software engineers to build digital products, you're at risk of falling behind in the new economy. If you work for an employer who operates in the old economy, you are increasingly at risk of professional irrelevance in the future.

The term *future of work* is often used in discussions about our technological transformation because it captures the confusion, change, and opportunity in three easy words. However, it's completely misleading. The future of work is already here.

While writing this chapter, I stumbled on a company that perfectly captures the future of work as it's happening now. The Pudding, a six-person startup, is an example of an organization that's evolving and augmenting traditional roles due to new technology. The company examines ideas through visual essays. They use data and research to communicate complex topics. They're a mashup of data engineers and journalists. Everything about their company and jobs is experimental. On their company website they describe the roles this way:

> *"Much of our work is done autonomously, with individuals choosing their essays and owning the whole*

story, from research to code. Each team member can do every step: research and reporting, data analysis, design, writing, and code."[21]

Everyone at The Pudding works as journalism engineers. They research. They code. They manipulate data. They tell fascinating stories. The result is incredible data visualizations that reframe how we understand stories. They've produced stories on everything from which rapper has the largest vocabulary in hip-hop (answer: Aesop Rock) to a visual history of Air Jordans to the Largest Ever Analysis of Film Dialogue by Gender Ever.

Their work is creative, data-driven, and interdisciplinary. They also pay well, especially compared to traditional journalism. According to PayScale, traditional editors make about $82,000 on the high end of salaries. Traditional journalist roles make $72,000 on the high end, $24,000 on the low end. Yet starting journalism engineers at The Pudding make $70,000 a year. Senior journalism engineers make $100,000. Editors at The Pudding make $115,000 year. I learned this because they're radically transparent about their salaries, posting them for everyone to see on their website, another move toward shaping a new world of work.

The future of work has already arrived

Asking if robots will take your job is really just like shouting into a Magic 8 Ball. There isn't a clear answer. The reality is far more

---

[21]The Pudding, "About."

nuanced than a bunch of robots showing up one day and saying, "Hey, give me your job."

If we ask our modern-day Magic 8 Ball, Google, if robots will take our jobs, the results range anywhere from *it is certain* to *my sources say no.* According to a 2017 Pew Research Survey, "...only three in 10 workers think it's at least somewhat likely that their own jobs will be mostly done by robots or computers during their lifetimes."[22] Yet we sure are nervous about the possibility. The same survey found that 72 percent of all Americans are worried about robots or computers taking over human work.

So, how do we make sense of a world filled with robot hype? To start, we have to acknowledge we're in a period of transition. While the Fourth Industrial Revolution isn't exactly on the tip of everyone's tongue, the rapid pace and scale of new technology will reshape the workplace in the next five years. Just because you don't see it happening doesn't mean it won't happen to you. In fact, if you happen to be a college educated American in a white-collar job, you're the most likely to think it won't happen to you. According to a 2017 Gallup survey of Americans' attitudes toward AI, 85 percent of Americans with a bachelor's degree or higher are not worried about their jobs becoming eliminated, compared to 72 percent of Americans without a bachelor's degree.[23] The problem with people in the 85 percent is that they're the most likely to drown in the technological tsunami headed our way because they weren't listening to the warnings.

---

[22]Pew, "Automation."
[23]Gallup, "Artificial Intelligence."

Robots in the workplace

Asking whether or not robots will take your job isn't helpful for career planning. The better question is: How will new technology augment your job in the near future? You must examine the ways in which new technology will change your job and ultimately your career path.

Whether or not a career path or job is at risk of being eliminated depends on the industry. The manufacturing and retail industry are at most risk of having robots displace workers. Amazon is leading the way in this. Amazon added an estimated 75,000 robots to its warehouses in 2017. It's estimated that robots will make up 20 percent of their employee base soon. Amazon, of course, is also famous for opening Amazon Go, a cashier-less store in Seattle. Showing proof of concept that a store may not need cashiers after all resulted in yet another flurry of articles about robots taking jobs. And what Amazon does, others follow, trying to keep up in a fiercely competitive business world.

Most of the focus right now on the future of work is on robots, in part because we can see them. Bright yellow robots moving palettes around a warehouse creates a nice visual for anyone reporting on the future of work. But that same visual causes those who don't work in warehouses, often those working in offices, to ignore the technology that's changing their workplace behind the scenes.

Artificial intelligence technology doesn't always present itself as bright yellow robots. Artificial intelligence is powered by advances in machine learning. AI usually takes the form of a seemingly benign software program that crunches a ton of data. Unless you are a machine learning engineer or data scientist, it's harder to see the technology's effect on the workplace.

Machine learning and artificial intelligence are used in the workplace to automate tasks to increase efficiency and productivity within an organization. Understanding these technologies is key to understanding how the workplace will change even if you can't physically see the technology shaping the change. This is the technology that will reshape the white-collar workforce and wreck the careers of the 85 percent of people who think it won't happen to them. The transformation will happen slowly yet cut deeply.

In June 2018, Bloomberg reported in an article titled "Amazon's Clever Machines Are Moving From the Warehouse to Headquarters," that Amazon's push to automate its workforce isn't just limited to the warehouse. Amazon had replaced the department that made decisions about inventory with a powerful automated platform that "predicts what shoppers want and how much to charge for it."[24] Amazon is a powerhouse in data collection. Data powers machine-learning technology, which gives a company the power to make predictive models that replace people. These are people who made six figures and likely had MBAs, given that Amazon hires the most MBAs of any company. Executives weren't spared either, as Bloomberg reported. They were moved around or chose to move out, many noting that they were unsurprised by the development.

Amazon makes the headlines, but stories like this pop up constantly if you know where to look. In Japan, Fukoku Mutual Life Insurance company replaced 34 of its workers with an automated system to calculate insurance payouts. The company estimated it'll save $1.2 million since they won't have to pay the salaries of the laid-off employees. They also anticipate it'll increase

---

[24]Bloomberg, "Clever Machines."

productivity by 30 percent. On Wall Street, Goldman Sachs has slowly replaced its traders with automated trading platforms, going from 600 in 2000, to just two in 2017.

In the first month of 2019, Accenture, a large, multinational consulting firm, publicized a new automation software, SynOps, that they used to automate 40,000 jobs to, "streamline and automate processes in areas such as finance and accounting, marketing, and procurement."[25] Accenture says nobody lost their jobs; they simply retrained those workers. Accenture is now selling this software to its clients to help them automate their systems and save money.

There are thousands of products built on AI technology that aim to do the work humans normally do in the workplace. From virtual AI assistants that schedule meetings to AI-powered chatbots that interview candidates to predictive algorithms that identify prospective sales candidates to algorithms that manage people, this technology is transforming our work and reshaping the workplace.

It's tempting to think you'll be spared because you're very good at your job. But this transformation isn't about talent; it's about cost. Companies are eager to use technology to replace work done by a human because it's cheaper for the company's bottom line. I write "a human" but it's actually hundreds of humans. After all, machines don't need breaks, vacation, health benefits, retirement contributions, raises, or stand-up desks. They also don't create productivity problems with coworkers when their lunch gets eaten from the communal fridge.

The effect of new technology in the workplace is more than having robot coworkers. For many, your job won't be eliminated

---

[25]Bloomberg, "Accenture."

outright by robots. Instead, the nature of work will shift and the skills required to stay relevant in your career will change. The result is that in five years, your current job may not look like the one you have now. And when you try to make a career change and apply for new jobs, you may find that you no longer have the required skills for the jobs you want.

The future is hybrid jobs

Thinking about the ways an employer will replace us with technology is a bit grim. But within this technological chaos is opportunity. The workplace transformation is creating hybrid jobs. Hybrid jobs are evolving from traditional roles and offer greater job and financial security in our new world of work.

Hybrid jobs are the roles of the new economy. In the report, "The 21st-Century Career," the multinational consulting firm Deloitte defined hybrid jobs as "jobs that create whole new job categories by mashing up disciplines."[26]

They continue: "These 'renaissance jobs' are those that combine technical expertise (in one or more domains) with expertise in design, project management, or client and customer interaction. They might be titled 'experience architect' or 'IoT engineer' or 'user experience designer' or 'security consultant,' and they typically involve knowledge of a technical domain, problem-solving capability, project management, and often industry expertise."

As employers change their business models, employees should change too. Changing careers offers you a chance to

---

[26]Deloitte Insights, "Changing Nature of Careers."

improve your professional life. How you define improvement is up to you. For many, improvement means more money and more job security. Hybrid jobs offer you both. The best-paying jobs that offer career security, outside of government jobs, are hybrid jobs. These job openings will be in roles that combine technical abilities, people skills, and domain expertise.

We already see the evolution to hybrid jobs happening. Digital designers are a hybrid job that's hiding in plain sight in most organizations. Over the last 15 years, graphic design roles have evolved into digital design roles. On top of understanding graphic design principles of color, layout, and typography, digital designers have a set of digital skills that cross an organization. Digital designers must understand user experience, wireframes, user flows, information architecture, and email marketing. They have HTML and CSS coding skills. JavaScript is a bonus. They also have power skills like creativity, collaboration, and communication that allow them to work across teams. For example, a digital designer at an ecommerce company must collaborate with different departments, requiring an understanding of sales funnels, marketing campaigns, and user data to inform design choices.

With a hybrid skill set, it is no wonder digital designers are paid well. According to PayScale, a digital designer's top salary is $78,000. On top of that, digital designers have the foundational digital skills that allow them to move into more specialized roles like interaction designer, which commands a top salary of $117,000.

The flip side of the digital designer's growth is that graphic designers without digital skills will find fewer opportunities in the marketplace over the next decade. They'll also make less than digital designers. The top salary of a graphic designer is $61,000.

Hybrid jobs come in all shapes and sizes. They defy traditional categories. With the introduction of artificial intelligence into the workplace, AI-adjacent roles are emerging as a type of hybrid job. AI-adjacent roles are the ultimate mashup job. They require technical knowledge, data fluency, communication skills, and industry domain knowledge.

The *New York Times* reported on how algorithms are changing traditional roles in the retail industry. In retail, fashion buyers who are normally tasked with making purchasing decisions, are increasingly using algorithms to do the task. These algorithms make fashion decisions by predicting the next big trend, a task normally associated with creative geniuses. With so much consumer data, predicting trends and stock levels is left to the machines, no intuition needed. The reporter shared how drastic the shift is:

> *"Retailers adept at using algorithms and big data tend to employ fewer buyers and assign each a wider range of categories, partly because they rely less on intuition...At Le Tote, an online rental and retail service for women's clothing that does hundreds of millions of dollars in business each year, a six-person team handles buying for all branded apparel—dresses, tops, pants, jackets."*[27]

The retail industry is using fewer buyers in the decision-making process. Instead, retailers are increasingly hiring people who can, "stand between machines and customers." These AI-adjacent roles

---

[27] *New York Times,* "White-Collar Work."

are filled by employees who understand the machines and the business needs.

Hybrid roles that require AI skills are on the rise. The research firm Burning Glass Technologies, found that almost 70,000 job postings in 2017 requested AI skills, a 252 percent growth over job postings in 2010. These jobs weren't all in the tech industry. Instead, they found "a wide range of industries including retail, health care, finance and insurance, manufacturing, information and professional services, technical services, and science/research."[28]

Hybrid jobs and AI adjacent roles might seem a bit out of reach from where you sit in your career. I assure you they are not. You can learn the skills and domain knowledge to get these jobs. Better yet, they're the jobs that will pay you better and position you as an in-demand worker among employers of the future.

It's not you, it's them

At this point you might be saying, "But I'm so good at my job." And you might very well be very good at your job. But consider this: companies value efficiency and productivity. Humans, even at their best, are not as productive and efficient as machines. Technology has advanced enough to give companies the ability to automate some of the work that humans do. Companies are doing the math and finding it cheaper to automate than to employ people.

Leaders of these companies have stated outright that they plan to eliminate jobs. The leader of Citibank declared in a 2018 interview that it will get rid of half of its 20,000 staff in technology

---

[28]Burning Glass Technologies, "Artificial Intelligence."

and operations over the next five years. Tim Thornsby, the CEO of Barclays, the massive global investment bank, put it this way in an interview in June 2018: "If your job involves a lot of keyboard hitting then you're less likely to have a happy future."[29]

That's some brutal advice from someone who just got $24 million to start his new job at Barclays. CEOs never talk about how they might be automated. Tim sounds like a jerk for saying that, but he's not wrong. He's simply translating the Fourth Industrial Revolution into terms we can understand.

Older workers are already experiencing the brutality of a rapidly changing workforce.

The *Wall Street Journal* recently wrote about the almost eight million older workers who are out of work despite a booming job market. They are formerly skilled workers who can't find a job. The article profiles an environmental engineer with a bachelor's degree who has sent out over 400 résumés without getting hired. He has faced years of unemployment. Age discrimination is part of the issue. But there's another factor at play: his skills are less relevant in today's market. He lacks the digital fluency to land middle- to high-paying jobs. He and many like him are stuck with part-time, temporary jobs that don't pay the bills or offer health benefits.

If you don't understand how new technology is used or possess digital literacy skills, you're at risk of becoming less valuable in the workforce. Think of older employees you've met who struggle with email, phone conferencing, or PDFs. That might be you in your later thirties or forties, struggling with basic machine-learning technology but far from retirement age. The technological revolution we're experiencing right now is bigger

---

[29]MarketWatch, "Big Banks."

than the digital revolution, which took us from analog to digital. It requires digital and data fluency, adaptability, and rethinking of the skills we need to be successful in our careers.

You weren't raised to think about how your skills would diminish in value by the time you're 30 or 40. But we're in a new world of work now and all of us must think like mini-futurists to navigate our careers. To succeed, you must adapt, not react, to changes in the workplace.

The Agile Worker

Agile: able to move quickly and easily.

The *New York Times* recently profiled Ms. Sow, a woman whose work exemplifies our new world of work. In her interview with the *New York Times*, Ms. Sow struggles to define a single job title that captures what she does. She's a producer, writer, podcaster, connecter, strategist, and influencer. Her work history defies traditional career paths:

> *"I don't think there's a title for what I do," is how Aminatou Sow, 33, describes her career, which takes many forms. Certainly, she is best known for hosting* Call Your Girlfriend, *a podcast devoted to sprawling conversations with her friend and collaborator Ann Friedman. Its popularity, with 6.1 million downloads in 2017, led to a live tour that sold out shows in New York, Washington, San Francisco, and Boston this fall, and the pair are writing a book,* Big Friendship, *for release in 2020. But Ms. Sow, who lives in Brooklyn*

*and speaks five languages, also works as a digital con-
sultant and strategist for brands such as Smartwater
and State Farm. Previously, she was at Google, run-
ning marketing for the company's civic initiatives. She
also moderates panels and does live interviews with
public figures, including Hillary Clinton and the gym-
nast Aly Raisman, and she co-founded Tech LadyMa-
fia, a network that links women working in the digital
economy. When Ms. Sow is pressed to come up with
one single job title that encompasses all she does, she
looks back at the last year, figures out what category of
work made her the most money, and says she is that.
Last year, that made her a digital strategist.*[30]

Ms. Sow is the future of work. She has multiple talents and
areas of knowledge. Her skill set is fluid, allowing her to apply
her diverse skills when new opportunities arise. Agile workers
like her are creative and collaborative. They stay one step ahead
of the game, looking to the future for inspiration and possibility.

You don't have to be as high profile as Ms. Sow to embrace an
agile career. However, you must shift from the old-school model,
where careers are defined by job titles and degrees to one where
careers are shaped by what you're able to do.

The curious opportunist

As you start the career change process, shift from the traditional
career ladder mindset to the agile worker mindset. An agile

---

[30] *New York Times,* "Aminatou Sow."

worker customizes their career path. They focus on skills, not job titles. Agile workers seek out people who excite and inspire them, learning from new perspectives. They build deep domain experience. Once they have a hold of it, they seek the next opportunity, whether it exists or not.

The agile worker is comfortable with ambiguity. They don't have to have it all figured out to make a step forward. They can experiment with a new job and, if it doesn't work, they know how to find a new opportunity.

The fabulous thing about the agile worker mindset is that if you wanted to become a data scientist or develop your communication skills to make an impact on climate change policy, you could start the process tomorrow. The agile worker framework gives you permission to change. Agile workers aren't limited by their major in college or intimidated by learning new skills.

The agile worker mindset gives you space to embrace and explore your curiosity. If, through the process of discovery, you decided that data science or communications wasn't your thing, the agile framework gives you space to start over and learn more.

Curiosity is your career BFF

My first "real job" after graduating from college was in a mind-numbingly boring role at a Fortune 500 company. I was a faceless worker in a sea of cubicles tasked with doing data entry for eight to 10 hours a day. As we approached the end of the quarter, we were required to work mandatory overtime, which meant 14 hours a day of data entry. It was the kind of place where we had meetings about upcoming meetings, and middle management fought each other to prove who could micromanage us the hardest.

As I plodded through days at the bottom of the Corporate America food chain, I sunk into a deep funk. I am part of a generation that was raised to think a college degree was the path to my dream job. I expected to graduate and sail into a job that merged my passions with big paychecks. The job I landed after graduation was the opposite of my passion. My passion was foreign languages and cultures, not checking the accuracy of hundreds of zip codes on fulfillment orders all day.

But I wasn't the only one in a funk. Few people in my 50+ person department were following their passion. I know because I asked. I wanted to understand why people chose to work in such a soulless place. I learned people liked getting paid and the free lunch we got daily. But the work? Nobody mentioned passion. Instead they talked about paychecks with overtime.

One of my favorite coworkers, a salty British woman who took no shit, explained to me why passion was overrated. For 20 years she'd owned a bar in England. It was her dream to open up a bar. For several years she loved it. Then she began to hate it. The constant cleaning. The drunks. The zombie working hours. When she moved to the States, she was thrilled to get a job that wasn't in a bar. At our job she got good benefits, worked during the day, and didn't have to deal with drunks. Overseeing fulfillment accounts wasn't her passion at all. She loved that the job gave her plenty of time to hang out with her grandkids.

It was the first time someone had reframed for me the idea that a job didn't have to be your passion. I grew up with parents who worked jobs that didn't align with their passions. They worked in casinos as craps dealers, as bartenders, and as administrative assistants. My mom made me learn how to type so I could fall back on receptionist jobs in case times were hard (and I did).

But I was still raised with the idea that all I had to do was merge my passion and work, and career magic would just happen.

Over the course of my career I've met tons of people who weren't following their passion yet were content in their work. When I was an administrative assistant, I wondered how other admins found passion in their work. Again, I asked. Their answers surprised me. Most weren't using the word passion to describe their work. Some admins felt good about helping management keep their shit together. They knew the executives couldn't function without them. They felt good using their organization skills to keep management on track and therefore keep the company functioning.

One of my favorite coworkers at this job, a mischievous woman who could sweet talk anyone into doing a task, told me she loved her job because she didn't have to take her work home with her. She felt sorry for management because she saw their stress, the late nights, and the "always-on mentality." She loved that she could do her job well and leave by 4 p.m. without the need to think about work until 7 a.m. the next day. She laughed when I asked if her job was her passion. "Of course not," she said. She had hobbies. That's where her passion lived.

The crushing pressure of passion

The push to find passion in our work stems in part from the American obsession with happiness. In the book *America the Anxious: How Our Pursuit of Happiness is Creating a Nation of Nervous Wrecks*, author Ruth Whippman notes that the selling of happiness-related products and services is estimated around $10 billion. Americans are in constant pursuit of happiness, and our workplaces are not exempt. If we must work so hard, we should be happy doing it, the thinking goes.

On top of that, we also equate hard work with morality. We get down on ourselves for not being productive on weekends and compete with each other to be the busiest. We also take less vacation compared to other countries. (How we can find happiness without taking loads of vacation is something I will never understand.)

In a country that values productivity and the pursuit of happiness it makes sense that we'd create a narrative that encourages us to seek the ultimate happiness in our work. And what can make you happier than fulfilling your passion on a daily basis and getting paid for it? It's a little easier to swallow the intense pressure to always be seeking happiness in your job by wrapping the idea in the nicely packaged career advice to "follow your passion."

Telling someone to follow their passion creates a lot of unnecessary pressure on career choices. We can't be expected to follow our passion at all times. Some people are in career transition, working mediocre jobs just to pay the bills or take care of family. The priority isn't passion. It's money to survive. There's no need to be down on yourself during those times for not following your passion.

We also change our minds. We talk about finding our passion as if there's only one true passion in life. Yet we are not the same person at 25, 35, and 45 and that's mighty okay. Our lives and priorities evolve. At 25 all I wanted was a job in a foreign country where I could dance until 5 a.m. and not fall behind on my student loans. By 35 I wanted a job with a competent boss, 100 percent company-paid benefits, and independence (I had two out of the three—bosses are always a crapshoot). Priorities change and so does our passion. Some of us have multiple passions. Choosing a single passion fills many with career FOMO (fear of missing out).

On top of that, work doesn't need to be a pleasure. Our obsession with passion glosses over the day-to-day grind that is work life. Even if you've found your true passion in work, there are lulls in the journey: inboxes that overflow, coworkers who make your life difficult, or organizations that lose funding. Contrary to the popular saying, *If you follow your passion, you'll never work a day in your life,* you can burn out on your passion. Sometimes our passions just don't make for viable work and we have to make hard tradeoffs.

Our work life is full of contradictions that make following your passion difficult. You can look forward to seeing your favorite coworkers while hating your boss. You can love your job while still being frustrated at the lack of opportunity for growth. You can make a ton of money and loathe the people you work with.

None of this is to say that you shouldn't seek joy or purpose in your job. Finding fulfillment in your work is important. Work that has a positive impact, connects you to interesting people, or challenges you intellectually are all elements of fulfillment. Work can be enjoyable without passion. But fulfillment and passion are not the same thing. It's possible to find meaning and joy in jobs you're not 100 percent passionate about.

As you start your career jump, give yourself permission to not find your passion. Or, if you've found your passion before but lost it, give yourself permission to change your mind. You are allowed to change your mind. Even Ivy League MBAs who spend $100,000 on a path to a new career change their minds. When I worked at Yale School of Management, I'd get calls from recent graduates in prestigious consulting or banking roles. Some had pursued an MBA specifically to follow their passion for investment banking or consulting, and it turned out they hated it. They wanted out but didn't know where to go without passion as a driver. They were stuck because they couldn't find their passion.

After tens of thousands of lines of data entry in cubicle world, I started getting curious about other opportunities. I didn't know what I wanted. But I knew I didn't want to stay in Corporate America. So, I started where any person starts: Google. I started reading about topics that interested me. I most definitely did this research on corporate time. My curiosity about life outside off the corporate America career path led me down a week-long Google rabbit hole. Eventually I landed on a website about graduate schools abroad. I didn't know graduate school abroad was an option for Americans. I never met anyone who had done it. I was super curious about living in a foreign country. Fast forward two years, and I was in Denmark on a fully paid scholarship in graduate school. I wasn't following my passion when I Googled. I was following my curiosity.

Curiosity trumps passion

In 2009, NASA held a nationwide contest for students to name their new Mars rover. The winning entry came from Clara Ma, a 12-year-old, who submitted the name Curiosity. In her essay she shared why she chose the name:

> *"Curiosity is an everlasting flame that burns in everyone's mind. It makes me get out of bed in the morning and wonder what surprises life will throw at me that day. Curiosity is such a powerful force. Without it, we*

wouldn't be who we are today. Curiosity is the passion that drives us through our everyday lives. We have become explorers and scientists with our need to ask questions and to wonder."[31]

Clara Ma articulated the beauty of curiosity better than any 12-year-old I've ever met. At 12 years old, I rode my bike off the back of a pickup truck and broke my collarbone. I was an idiot who couldn't articulate much beyond my love for the show *Beverly Hills, 90210.* Let this be a reminder that we all take different paths in life.

The advice to follow your passion serves one important purpose: to push us toward meaning in our career. But this advice also has another effect: it keeps us stuck. Plenty of people toil away in jobs wondering what their passion is, unable to move until they find it.

There is a better option. Instead of following your passion, follow your curiosity. Curiosity is an act of seeking. Curiosity asks you to investigate the professional world around you. Our careers shouldn't be stationary. They evolve. They change shapes. Much like the Mars rover, which seeks out new terrain and then communicates its findings, you must do the same in your career.

Better yet, curiosity doesn't put pressure on you. We're all naturally curious. You have questions about how things work. I'd be willing to bet you're pretty curious about the future, because you picked up this book. Curiosity motivates you to seek out the ideas and work that interest you.

---

[31]NASA, "Curiosity."

The best part: you don't have to wait to find your curiosity. In the context of your career, curiosity asks us to question what's possible. Embracing curiosity drives you forward in your career even if you don't know what motivates you. Use it as a tool for exploration and understanding. It comes in mighty handy when you don't know which direction to go with your career. Instead of asking, "What is my passion?" shift the question. Inject more curiosity.

- What kinds of jobs exist that use my skills and experience?
- What type of work interests me and how do I get those jobs?
- What are the backgrounds of people who work in (insert interesting work here)?
- What types of companies hire people with my interests?

Broaden your idea of what makes a career, because there is so much more to your career than passion. Explore the type of work you enjoy, coworkers who motivate you, and workplaces that interest you. Look at possibilities beyond passion as the world of work changes. Prioritizing curiosity over passion ensures you don't miss out on opportunities and paths that open up new passions.

Discover the Possible Jobs

In 2012, I shifted careers from a student advising job at a university into a luxury travel writing job. I hustled my way into a role as a full-time travel writer for a private jet tour company. In my role as a private jet writer I was definitely out of my element. I was expected to write about the private jet lifestyle even though I'd never even stayed in a luxury hotel. But I can write, and so I did. I wrote about relaxing in the overwater bungalows in the Maldives and hot air balloon rides at sunrise over the Namibian sand dunes. Of course, I never did these any of things. I just learned how to write about them as if I'd traveled right alongside our guests in our fancy private jet, sipping champagne and eating exquisite meals coated in gold dust (pretty sure that's what rich people do).

One day I interviewed a staff member for a blog post. He had been to over 120 countries. As we talked, I learned about a job that I never knew existed: a travel scout. This man's job was to travel to new, increasingly exotic places to see if these places could host our tours. The places needed to have upscale yet personalized amenities and accommodate a group of around 75 people. He'd travel to the places, stay in the luxury hotels, try the activities. Then he'd write a report for the product team back at the office with recommendations. It was a sweet gig. It is a job that's similar to a location scout, a role common in television and ad agencies. Location scouts find ideal places that evoke the right feel and setting for a TV or photography shoot. Travel scouts find ideal places for tour groups.

As a language major in college, I sought jobs that would let me travel. The only options I heard were teaching English abroad and becoming a flight attendant. I wish someone had told me about travel scouts. This type of job is rarely advertised. It's a job that people grow into over time, not an entry-level position. I was jealous. I had the job with the title that many people wanted: private jet travel writer. Yet all I wanted was the travel scout job.

I never got a job as a travel scout. But learning about a job that I didn't know existed changed how I thought about my career path. It introduced me to the concept of possible jobs.

Emerging possible jobs and career paths

Possible jobs are jobs that you discover but didn't know existed. Often these jobs pop up on your radar when you're in the middle of another career. They grab ahold of you and say, "Hey, wouldn't it be cool if you spent your working days doing this?" Possible jobs can be your dream job. Or they can just be a good job that launches you into a new career path. It takes curiosity, an openness to conversation, and a dash of imagination to find possible jobs. But once you know how to look for them, you'll realize they're hidden in plain sight.

Lost in all the headlines about robots taking jobs are all the *possible jobs*. Possible jobs include the new jobs and career paths that artificial intelligence and machine learning technology create.

As organizations experiment with new technology, the jobs that get the work done will change. When new jobs are added it creates a ripple effect. With 133 million new jobs projected for the future of work comes an unquantifiable number of jobs that will have to change to support these new roles. These yet-to-exist jobs are a flashing neon sign pointing you toward the future. It's pointing to a different path, one that's filled with experiments and new careers. It's a path for the agile worker, one who's curious about possibilities.

One example of possible jobs is the emerging field of conversation design. Use of voice assistants like Google Home, Siri, and Alexa, are on the rise among consumers. Conversation designers create and shape the interactions you have with voice assistants. Companies need conversation designers to build engaging interactions that make happy customers. A good conversation designer is a person who understands the technology and people. The conversation designers work together with engineers to improve the user experience, resulting in a better product and more intelligent tools. People who work as conversation designers must understand people, language, and user needs. They must be relentlessly curious about how this technology shapes our daily lives. It helps to have familiarity with the technology, but they don't have to be an AI engineer to design conversations.

Conversation design is just one among thousands of *possible jobs* for the future. The path to becoming a conversation designer is full of possibility. It takes a curious person who's willing to add new skills to their current experience. Many times, those are new skills that don't fit into a traditional role.

The possible jobs of the future require an interdisciplinary skill set. You can't just be a numbers person. Or a people person. Or a person who only works with engineers. These silos inhibit your ability to work in emerging careers. Instead, you must collect skills across disciplines and work across silos.

The future is yours. It belongs to those who want to rise up and seize it. Every day there are new roles and opportunities to create, build, lead, and experiment with work. In all this change, there are so many possibilities. And you can be part of it.

CHAPTER 3

The Upskill Revolution

Alexa, why does a baby boomer who doesn't read emails, won't update their browser version, and can't rotate a PDF make triple my salary?
—tweet by @tony_charm on July 23, 2018[32]

The first time I saw this tweet I giggled my face off. I was not surprised that this viral tweet had at least 42,000 retweets and 203,000 likes when I checked it. It perfectly captures the rants that are shared between friends and coworkers throughout our collective workplaces. Our generation is mad that older generations in management are raking in the money and refusing to change while we're forced to do all the things with stagnant wages. Of course, I'm paraphrasing years of happy hour rants and coaching sessions filled with people unloading about the many reasons they hated their jobs. But it's not news to anyone in the workplace that the tension between generations is real. Much of the younger generation's gripes revolve around money,

---

[32]@tony_charm (Twitter), "Alexa."

leadership's inflexibility, and the perception that our managers from different generations haven't put in the time to learn new skills. It's pretty spicy in the workplace with four generations all trying to work together.

After I shared the tweet with all my friends, I remembered a podcast I'd heard about the future of work. The podcast featured Susan Lund, a partner at McKinsey Global Institute, talking about the need for lifelong learning:

> *"The time it takes for people's skills to become irrelevant will shrink. It used to be, 'I got my skills in my 20s; I can hang on until 60.' It's not going to be like that anymore. We're going to live in an era of people finding their skills irrelevant at age 45, 40, 35. And there are going to be a great many people who are out of work."* [33]

I realized that the tweet by *@tony_charm* could easily be targeted at me and my friends in the next 10 years. I'm 15 years out of my undergraduate degree. I have a master's degree. But I am not part of a younger generation who grew up learning how to code. I have a diverse set of skills, in part because I've spent my adult life reinventing my professional self. But even I'm not safe from the youth. Computer science degrees and training are so hot right now that universities can't keep up. The *New York Times* reports that, "The number of undergraduates majoring in the subject more than doubled from 2013 to 2017, to over 106,000." [34]

---

[33] McKinsey & Company, "Automation."
[34] *New York Times*, "Computer Science."

I've written a lot about the software that is reshaping our jobs. But the youth are coming too. And they're going to have the skills that many of us, who are further along in our careers, do not have.

Thanks to the fear of the youth, I started upskilling. It started with my curiosity about AI. I began by reading about algorithms and their impact on people and the workplace. I made a career jump into a job at an AI startup so I could learn how AI-powered products are built and the ethical considerations. Now I'm taking online courses about artificial intelligence and started learning Python, the programming language for data scientists and machine learning engineers.

As I write this book, I'm trying to beat the youth and the robots by upskilling. Upskilling is now the new normal in our careers.

Upskilling is learning

Upskilling is the pursuit of formal and informal learning experiences to build new skills and upgrade your career. Upskilling is a strategy to keep your skills updated as the workplace changes. It also helps you compete with the machines and the youth.

When you upskill, you build new skills on top of your existing skills. You also learn the industry vocabulary and domain knowledge to complement your new skills.

The process of learning new skills, or reskilling, plays a major role in your career change. To gain new skills for your career jump, you need to upskill. There are many ways to upskill, from taking courses online to bootcamps to college degree programs. But the path to upskilling begins by reflecting on your existing skill set. Then identify your target job on your new career path and which skills are necessary to get that job. If you lack the necessary skills to qualify for that new career path, you can identify a learning experience that will teach you the missing skills.

For example, imagine you're a writer who wants to move on from the hustle of freelancing. You recently learned about virtual reality (VR). You're interested in becoming a producer for a VR film company so you can bring other people's stories to life in a VR startup. You already have strong creative, collaboration, and writing skills that you bring to the position. But you are missing design skills, industry knowledge, and experience collaborating with software engineers. So, you search for a learning experience that will help you upskill and learn how to design in VR environments. You sign up for an online course in 3D Interaction Design in Virtual Reality. You start participating in online webinars about the industry and going to meetups to hear experiences from people who work in the field. You've just created your own upskill path.

While upskilling is critical for career-changers, it doesn't have to be a big undertaking. There are many ways to upskill that don't involve going back to school. Maybe you're a librarian who learns how to fundraise so you can turn your advocacy into a full-time job. Maybe you're a manager who learns how to analyze data so you can make better decisions about your team. Sometimes upskilling is just the process of collecting a new skill that makes you a more agile employee.

Rather than waiting for your employer to train you or assuming your degree bestowed everything you need to know for the rest of your professional life, upskilling is a proactive approach to staying relevant in your career.

Upskilling also gives you the power to claim your space in a rapidly changing world. New technology and new jobs open up opportunity. Right now, the new world of work is dominated by those with access, privilege, and money. Upskilling allows you to learn cutting-edge skills and claim your space in this new world of work.

For example, if you're a social worker, you're likely quite good at relationship management, program management, and knowledge management. Learning how machine learning and predictive analytics affect policy would put you in a strong position to fight back against bad technology. Currently, local governments are experimenting with predictive algorithms and facial recognition technology that negatively impacts marginalized communities and criminalizes poverty. Taking an online course about artificial intelligence for people with nontechnical backgrounds, learning data analytics, or collaborating with software engineers or vendors who work on AI-related projects, could all be paths to upskilling. Your domain knowledge in social work and skills working within the system would be greatly enhanced by adding technical skills alongside a basic understanding of AI systems and predictive software.

As you upskill and collect new skills, you build momentum to position you for leadership. Whether you move up, diagonal, or jump into a new field entirely, upskilling will increase your ability to influence and make an impact inside organizations.

Domain knowledge vs. skills

If you have a college degree, you've gathered a ton of domain knowledge. Domain knowledge is a general knowledge about a specific topic, industry, or field.

Domain knowledge is necessary for a career jump. You need to understand the vocabulary and issues in your new field. But skills keep you employed and make you more money. I'm grateful for a college degree even though I'm still struggling with student loans. It has opened up more professional doors than would have been available without one. But, like a lot of liberal arts students, I was completely lost after college. I had no idea how to translate what I learned—the domain knowledge—into skills that were relevant for a career. It took me 10 years of work to figure out my skills.

Now I know my skills. My liberal arts degree taught me how to take massive amounts of qualitative data and make sense of it. I learned how to evaluate information and write well. Thanks to my liberal arts degree, I can analyze large amounts of information and talk about it to people. This skill is in high demand right now in the workforce. Analytics translators are people who can analyze patterns in data and explain it to others. They work with data scientists and management to ensure that insights gathered from the company's data are understood by decision makers. These people need communication skills plus technical knowledge to get that done. Analytics skills are easy to learn. Communication skills are much harder to learn.

College degrees are one ticket to better career opportunities in American society. But college doesn't teach you how to separate skills from domain knowledge. The result is that plenty of graduates either don't know their skills or overestimate what they can do because they have a degree that represents years of study. And those without a degree assume they don't have marketable skills, when, in fact, they do.

Skills are your currency in the new world of work

"Coding is like writing, and we live in a time of the new industrial revolution. What's happened is that maybe everybody knows how to use computers, like they know how to read, but they don't know how to write." —*Susan Wojcicki*[35]

We've evolved from a system in which a degree meant a steady career path with clear job titles and progression. Career progress is no longer about hitting that next job title. It's about your abilities. Employers are asking candidates, "What can you do? What skills have you used in the past that show you can do this job?" That's very different from asking, "What degree do you have that qualifies you for this job?"

A skill is simply an ability. In every job, you apply a skill to complete a task. No matter your role or level of work, you bring a set of skills to your work to get the job done. Ideally, an employer pays you according to how your skills are valued in the market. Unfortunately, not all skills are valued equally in American culture. That's why the real hard work like waiting tables, caring for the elderly, or parenthood pays so little—or nothing at all—despite requiring a considerable amount of skill.

It's important to state that your current job title and wage doesn't reflect your actual work abilities. I've worked with plenty of administrative assistants without a college degree making $30,000 year. These admins juggle competing priorities, navigate challenging personalities, and write charming emails that get shit done far better than the software engineers making $100,000 who can't even engage in a conversation. I know mothers who

---

[35] *Financial Times*, "Susan Wojcicki."

can reschedule a friend date while entertaining a child and mentally working through a company presentation for the next day. I think of them every time an executive falls to pieces when their PowerPoint doesn't work.

I tell you this because your skills aren't defined by your job title or education. They aren't limited by the title assigned to you in your current job. As a career-changer who wants a better career that pays more and offers more opportunity and security for the future, you have to speak the language of skills. Skills are the currency of the future of work.

Power Skills for money and job security

As an agile worker, your professional goal is to collect skills, not job titles. You want to be so versatile that you can adapt and bounce back from any unforeseen layoff, recession, or robot-pocalypse. Agile workers collect Power Skills. Power Skills are the abilities that allow you to move seamlessly through the new world of work. They give you the flexibility to change careers and find work that fits your lifestyle. Master the Power Skills and you'll find that opportunities open up for you. Most importantly, Power Skills get you the jobs that pay well.

Power Skills aren't limited to a single role. Instead, they're cross-functional skills. Employers are clamoring to find candidates with Power Skills.

You likely already have a few Power Skills. Your career change is an opportunity to collect even more. But don't limit your collection time to career changes. Agile employees collect Power Skills throughout their careers, ensuring they stay relevant and in demand. Everyone has the ability to build Power Skills by upskilling and learning on the job.

The following Power Skills are those you need to thrive in the new world of work. As you review the skills below, think about your work experiences. What skills do you already have? Which ones do you need to build? Which ones would you like to get better at? Don't worry about how to build those skills just yet. I'll show you how in the next chapter.

Communication

This is a massive bucket of skills. Communication skills include your ability to write for different contexts, communicate new ideas, speak publicly, take feedback, and listen to colleagues. Communication skills are the abilities most people think they have, but don't. If you've ever had a boss who talked *at* you, you know this isn't communication. It's simply talking at your face. If you've ever received a 500-word jargon-filled email from management, you've experienced bad communication.

Skilled communicators understand their audience and deliver information in a way that their audience will understand. In the workplace, good communicators can persuade an audience of 500 people, translate data into an engaging story that management understands, and write emails people actually read. Communication skills also involve active listening, which includes an openness to having conversations and diverse perspectives.

Employers consistently rank communication skills as the number one skill they are looking for in a job. Pair this Power Skill with technical skills, and you'll be an in-demand employee.

Systems Thinking

Your organization is a complex system. Understanding how your work fits into your team's goals and the company as a whole is a critical skill. Systems thinking is understanding how complex systems work. Engaging in systems thinking means getting outside your professional box. It's the ability to look behind the scenes and beyond what you can see in your everyday work. It requires asking curious questions about the work you do and paying attention to other people's roles inside the organization. It also means understanding the processes that make the place run.

For example, if you're an IT professional, learning about business objectives helps you find new IT solutions that improve business outcomes. If you're a creative person working on a team, learning about how the budget works could help you find savings in creative buys.

Systems thinking helps you understand complexity and then break it down into manageable parts. Systems thinking teaches you to ask curious questions. You learn how to find opportunities to implement new ideas and seek out people whose work complements yours. And employers love that shit.

Knowledge Management

People who are skilled in knowledge management know how to make sense of the large amount of information available to them. They're also ridiculously resourceful. In the new world of work, knowledge is everywhere. Knowing how to curate information and share what is relevant with the right people is an in-demand skill. Your ability to make sense of the knowledge produced in your place of work and translate it into documents, presentations, or processes makes you an invaluable worker. It raises your profile inside a company and helps you build relationships.

Knowledge management is also a Power Skill for your career change. Evaluating and managing your learning experiences is part of upskilling. Communicating the results and impact of your learning experience to your future employer is a reflection of your knowledge management skills.

Digital Fluency

Adapting to new digital tools is key to staying relevant in the workplace. Digital fluency is the ability to navigate software and communication platforms in the workplace. It's the ability to learn new software systems instead of shying away from them. Employees and managers who say, "Technology, amirite?" every time they encounter a new piece of technology in the workplace lack digital fluency.

Digital fluency also means understanding code. You don't have to become a software developer or build your own app. But you need to understand the logic of programming, the basic syntax, and use cases for popular programming languages.

Communication technology is always evolving. Messaging apps, video tools, and communication platforms change how we collaborate, manage, and connect. Learning how to build relationships effectively using these tools is important as organizations embrace remote work and distributed teams.

Building digital fluency requires a curious mindset that seeks out opportunities to learn new technology and understand its impact on the organization and people.

Data Fluency

Data fluency is another big bucket. At its core, it's the ability to understand how to acquire data and make sense of it. That includes asking the right questions about data, identifying data collection methods, and cleaning raw data. It's also analyzing data and transforming it into stories that your audience understands. Data analytics can't help your organization if people can't understand the findings.

You don't have to be a data scientist to work with data. It takes a village to source and transform data so that it creates a meaningful impact. Data fluency is already a must-have skill for management and increasingly entry-level roles. Understanding how the organization that you work for collects and uses data to improve their business, services, or products, is an essential Power Skill. It's also the ticket to better-paying jobs.

Creativity

Creative people bring new solutions to organizations struggling with complex problems. Employers need creative people more than they need people who show up and follow directions. They need people with bold ideas. They want people with creative ways to implement those ideas. They hire people who can create with others from different backgrounds.

Creativity is mental agility plus the willingness to look at problems from new angles. Contrary to popular belief, creativity isn't reserved for people who are naturally creative or have art skills. Creativity is a skill that's developed, curated, and applied. It happens when people put themselves in new environments and expose themselves to views that differ from their own.

Employees who merge creative backgrounds with communication and technical skills are going to be unstoppable in the future of work.

Collaboration

Agile employees don't work in silos. They work across teams. Collaboration is the ability to produce work with people whose ideas and perspectives differ from yours. It's approaching your work with an interdisciplinary mindset and acknowledging there's more than one way to approach a problem.

Collaboration is more than meeting with people. It's being an active listener in discussions. Collaborating means receiving and giving feedback to make the work you do better. It's also an ability to work with others whose backgrounds differ from yours to produce impactful results.

Problem Solving

As digital transformation takes place, problems get complicated fast. Problem solving is the ability to think through solutions, test new ideas, learn from them, and keep moving forward. It's the ability to question assumptions, seek potential solutions, and discuss them with others. Problem solving isn't a stand-alone skill. It's the combination of communication and collaboration, with a dash of systems thinking thrown in. It's another skill that people think they have, but often don't.

Collect Power Skills

Power Skills help you level up your career. They make you a more agile employee while ensuring you're providing value in any company. Better yet, Power Skills protect you from automation in the workplace. Collect Power Skills and nurture them as you evolve in your career. They ensure you stay relevant in a skill-based economy and they'll position you for the possible jobs that might not even exist yet.

The Path Forward

Our careers have changed dramatically from those of our parents. New technology and business models are bringing a change to the workforce that will leave many underskilled and unprepared. The future belongs to those who collect skills and apply them in new environments.

While all this change can seem a bit bleak, there are more opportunities to learn new skills than ever before. Seize this time as yours and prepare for your career jump. The path forward requires an agile mindset, one that imagines the possibilities among all the chaos and change. Instead of waiting for the right career path to find you, create your own path.

We've reached a pivotal point in the book. This is the part where you start to take action. I'm going to show you how to move forward and get unstuck. But we can't have all work and no play. It's time for an intermission.

PART TWO

An Adventurous Intermission

CHAPTER 4

Imagination Station

As a kid in the '80s, I read a lot of Choose Your Own Adventure books. I loved the ridiculousness of these stories and how you could die from something absurd at any wrong page turn. Recently, I picked up a CYOA book at Powell's Books, the famous bookstore in Portland, Oregon. I gave it a go and ended up crushed to death in a cave, locked in the spider's giant hairy legs. I still love the ridiculous endings. I also love changing my mind if I picked the wrong path.

As I reread the stories to try different paths, I realized this is exactly how our careers should be as we work to adapt to our new world of work. Yet, as we grow and settle into our professional lives, we are less likely to start over, even if we're facing a dead-end career or unpleasant environment. The more experienced we get in our careers, the more we cling to certainty, avoiding ambiguous paths.

To successfully change a career, you have to navigate that ambiguity. You have to claim your own path and move yourself forward without a guarantee that it'll work out exactly like you plan.

The author of the original CYOA books was trying to change the way kids read. The online publication Mental Floss describes the CYOA books this way: "Every few pages, he or she had to make a critical decision on how to proceed. There were about 40 possible endings, with some paths leading to glory and others ending in alien invasion, tyrannosaurus attack, and other forms of ruin."[36]

My friends, this is exactly like your career. Some of you will end up in glory. You might become a successful CEO with a private jet or a VP of a global organization whose impact transforms society. You might end up a notch below leadership, as a critical person who works behind the scenes to make sure everything gets done. Or you might be a person who lives a pretty chill work life and has time for family and hobbies. Your path might bounce between continents or roles that bring you immense joy, without status or salary. While nobody will get eaten by a tyrannosaur or battle an alien invasion, some will end up in dire circumstances. That's the nature of careers. They are full of choices. There is no single path to career success because success is defined on your terms.

CYOA books were designed to empower kids to make the choices instead of the author making them. As the publisher of the first CYOA books explained to Mental Floss, "The reading happened because kids were put in the driver's seat. They were the mountain climber, they were the doctor, they were the deep-sea explorer."[37]

In this book, I'm putting you in the driver's seat of your career. You have always had the power to make the decisions. I'm just showing you how to find and shape the path you want.

---

[36]Mental Floss, "Choose Your Own Adventure."
[37]Ibid.

The future of work belongs to those who can navigate the unknown and make choices without knowing how it will all turn out. The career ladder, with its clear paths upward and promise of success, is no longer. Instead, we're navigating a chess board of opportunities where we can be any player we want in our careers. And that's far more exciting than a boring-ass career ladder.

In this book, I want you to change how you think about careers and take control of your career path. Our work lives are filled with chaos and decision points. Experimenting with career choices helps you navigate the career chaos in the new world of work. But more importantly, as a career-changer, you need to harness your imagination. I want you to imagine all the possible outcomes and career paths as you start your career change. I want you daydreaming about possibilities.

So, in the spirit of CYOA books, this intermission is a workplace story where you get to experiment with the outcomes. Just like your career, you'll make many choices in this story that will shape the outcome. There is no right choice in this story. You might find a new career that gives you all the money. Or you might learn that your job is being automated. Or you might end up with a cubicle mate who eats tuna fish sandwiches every day at their desk for lunch. Just like in life, you can't predict the future.

Career changes are a series of small decisions and steps forward. The more comfortable you become with making decisions in the face of ambiguity, the easier it will be to change into a more impactful career.

If you're ready for the intermission, turn to the next page.
If you'd rather get down to the business of changing your career, turn to page 119

The Struggle Is Real

Your career is a struggle. You work at a mediocre job. The company is the opposite of inspiring. You've recently taken on more work because a coworker quit unexpectedly. Your boss doesn't pay much attention to you. You haven't had a raise in three years.

Each day you fantasize about getting fired from your job. Not because you want to get fired. You just don't know where to go from here. You can't decide what's worse: a job search or staying put in your mediocre job. You think that if they fired you, you'd have no choice but to look for a new job. You daydream about a new career, something that pays better, something less soul-crushing. You have no idea what career that would be.

You walk to the bathroom. You pass the daily announcements board. You read today's motivational quote:

> *"Make every detail perfect and limit*
> *the number of details to perfect."*
> *—Jack Dorsey.*

You roll your eyes. You contemplate writing your own motivational quote. You imagine writing in large letters: NOTHING YOU DO MATTERS HERE. You fantasize about getting caught and about not getting caught and gossiping with your coworkers about who did it.

You go to the bathroom and spend an ungodly amount of time on your phone. As you return to your desk, you pass the whiteboard again.

You see the markers. You feel the pull. Why not write your own motivational quote? You visualize it on the board:

NOTHING YOU DO MATTERS HERE.
—Management

If you decide to write it out on the whiteboard, turn to the next page.
If you are a professional who would never, ever write that on a whiteboard, turn to page 90.

WRITE ON THE WHITEBOARD

You write the phrase big and bold as quick as you can. You step back to admire your work. You take a photo and upload it to your Insta story, captioning it as #motivationalquote.

You return to your desk. You get an email 27 minutes later with "Incident" as the subject line. You click, eager to see it.

> *Team,*
>
> *We are aware of an incident occurring this afternoon near the Cascades conference room. Please be advised we are reviewing all employee sensor data to determine next steps. We encourage all employees to use proper communication channels when providing feedback about our organization.*
>
> *Regards,*
>
> *Management*

You panic. You didn't realize that your company had an employee monitoring system. You remember something from a meeting about new employee badges with sensors. You thought it was for a communication project not an employee data tracking system that monitors employee movements.

You refresh your emails and notice you're locked out of the system. You try to reset but the prompt says your user name doesn't exist. You smash the keys around some more. You look up to see your boss walking toward you with the two security guards who high five you each day as you scan in.

Your dreams are coming true: you're getting fired from your mediocre job.

To restart, turn to page 86.

To end the stories and learn how to change your career, turn to page 119.

YOU DON'T WRITE ON THE WHITEBOARD

You return to your desk, pleased with your impulse control. You may hate your job, but you are a professional after all. Your boss calls you into her office. She informs you that the company algorithm that monitors employee emails has indicated that you are unhappy.

You tell your boss that you are fine, thank you very much. She disagrees and says that the algorithm has been analyzing all your emails. The system has flagged your use of curse words as above average. Your employee happiness rank is a 2 out of 10. You see a sad face emoji next to your name.

You admit you've been a bit unhappy. Your boss assures you of their open door policy which reads like a corporate PR statement.

You leave the meeting, irritated that all your emails are being analyzed by your employer. You imagine working for a company that trusts you. Your friend told you recently that they're hiring at her startup. She keeps raving about the place, but you don't know anything about it. You should text her.

You're starving, so you decide to hit up the break room to see if any of yesterday's donuts are left. On the way, you see your boss's boss exiting a meeting. You've been emailing him your reports for the past three months, but you've never officially met in person. You think it would be a good chance to put a face to a name. You always hear that it's good to network.

If you decide to duck into the break room to avoid him, turn to page 91.
If you decide to network with your boss's boss, turn to page 94.

DUCK INTO BREAK ROOM

You duck into the break room. There are no donuts. Instead, there's a pile of paleo health bars courtesy of your wellness department. You read the attached note: A HEALTHY EMPLOYEE IS A PRODUCTIVE EMPLOYEE! You remember the kick-off campaign that encourages all employees to wear company-issued fitness bracelets that track their calories and exercise habits. You opted out because you don't think your employer should know what you do outside of the workday. Your employer punished you by withholding the $750 company health insurance contribution. So much for wellness.

You're angry now. You can't tell if it's from the hunger or remembering your high deductible. You take a bite of the paleo bar to ease the hangry and gag. It tastes like damp dust. Your coworker laughs watching your disgust. He tells you he wants to record your reaction and tag the company on Instagram.

If you decide to record a reaction video to another paleo bar, turn to page 92.

If you decide to text your friend like you originally planned, turn to page 93.

RECORD THE REACTION

You record the video, gagging again at the taste. You don't even need to exaggerate. Your coworker uploads it to his Insta and it goes viral by the end of the day. The next day you create the account @garbagebars, uploading a reaction review video for every free snack bar your wellness department offers.

Your Insta blows up, going from two followers to 600K in a week. You quit your job and become an Instagram influencer selling Tummy Tea for Strength at $5,000 a post.

You finally changed careers.

To restart, turn to page 86.

To end the stories and learn how to change your career, turn to page 119.

TEXT YOUR FRIEND

You text your friend to tell her that you're miserable in your job. You ask her what she likes about her job. She says that her favorite part of her work is that her boss gives her challenging projects and trusts her to get the work done. She says the company is a bit chaotic, not very well organized. You learn they have unlimited vacation, a budget for professional development, and people work from home once a week. You also learn that she makes more money than her last job.

You ask her if there are any jobs that are a fit for you. She tells you there might be some but that you'd need to be comfortable working with data and giving presentations.

You're terrified of public speaking but working from home and a raise is exactly what you need right now in your life. You tell her you could do it. You have no idea how, but you need an out.

You sign up for a self-paced data analytics course online offered for free through your current place of work. You start making small presentations to pass the days, getting a bit better at your presentations.

You do the work to learn new skills. Six months later, you're in a new career making $25,000 more than your last job and working from home with your dog once a week. Life is good.

To restart, turn to page 86.

To end the stories and learn how to change your career, turn to page 119.

YOU NETWORK

You walk over to your boss's boss and introduce yourself, reminding him your name is on the reports you send weekly. He smiles politely. You tell him a few ideas you have about improving the reporting process. You notice his deep tan as he tells you he's just returned from a conference in Portugal. Your manager told you just last week that there's no budget for raises this year. You make a mental note to ask about conferences in Portugal. He tells you he's late to a meeting and calls you Drew. Your name is not Drew.

As he leaves, a woman enters the office. You notice how she radiates lightheartedness and confidence. Your office radiates boredom. You watch the woman engage in a clever back and forth with your friend. You hope she isn't applying to your place of work. You don't want to see her spirit crushed.

You return to your desk and message your work bestie who works near the front desk.

```
You:     Who's visiting?
Friend:  Some consultant.
You:     I bet she makes more than us.
Friend:  She does. I saw the invoice
         with her hourly bill rate.
You:     What's her name?
```

You Google her name. Her LinkedIn profile says she's a user experience designer. You check Glassdoor to figure out how much she makes. You learn that the average user experience designer makes over $100,000. You realize that's double your salary. Your feelings turn to jealousy. You'd like to get paid for doing something other than people wrangling.

You spend the next 10 minutes scanning job descriptions for user experience designers. They're interesting but you're not qualified. You close your tabs, check your Insta, and head to a meeting.

You exit the door to your office and run right into the woman, stopping just before you collide. You feel transparent because you've just stalked her online. She laughs and asks if you're okay. You stare.

If you decide to ignore her and ghost your job, turn to page 96.
If you decide to talk to her, turn to page 97.

YOU GHOST

You don't want to spend another day in this place. You've heard about people ghosting their jobs before. You just didn't think you'd be one of those people.

You ignore her and walk right past the meeting room and out the door. As you exit, you wonder if there's a word in another language for the simultaneous feeling of panic, joy, and relief. You grab your phone. You send your last email to your boss and boss's boss with two simple words: I quit. You mouth the word *fuckers* as you hit send.

You don't know how you're going to explain this to your family, friends, or even your next employer. You start your drive, windows down, and all the glorious feelings wash over you. You realize you could drive Lyft for a while to get by. You'll have to cut back on your spending, but you'll get some flexibility in your schedule to sort out your next move.

Four months later, one of your Lyft passengers compliments you on your playlist. She tells you she founded a startup direct-to-fan music platform. You tell her you've talked with so many musicians while driving Lyft. She gives you her contact info and tells you to follow up because she might have a business development job for you. She compliments your conversational skills. You tell her that after four months of driving strangers, you've learned how to talk to anyone.

You envision a new path in the music industry and it makes you smile. You don't know how this will turn out but you're going to explore it.

To restart, turn to page 86.
To end the stories and learn how to change your career, turn to page 119.

YOU TALK TO HER

You ask her if she's new to the building. She says yes. She's a consultant tasked with helping your benefits department design a better app. You ask if she can design an app that lowers your deductible. Your timing is off. You smile through the awkwardness.

She laughs anyway and says she'll work on it. She asks what you do. You debate telling her that all you do is watch YouTube videos and ignore emails from people you don't like until you can ghost out of the office at the end of the day.

You tell her you're responsible for compiling all metrics across departments and writing a weekly report for management. She asks you why your company hasn't built an internal dashboard that does that automatically. You hadn't thought about that before.

You realize your job could be automated.

If you choose to get mad at her for suggesting you're replaceable, turn to page 98.
If you choose to ask her a question about her job, turn to page 99.

YOU GET MAD

You tell her that's a ridiculous idea. You tell her that no computer software could do what you do. You state proudly that you've been at the company for five years. You tell her how much your boss values you. You wish her good day and storm off.

You continue to your first meeting. Your boss and her boss are there along with the IT department. The meeting begins. Your boss announces that they're building a new system to automate reporting across departments. They envision a dashboard where management can view each department's metrics in real time. He smiles at you and tells you that you're a valuable asset. You were asked to join the meeting so everyone on the project can understand how you compile reports.

You realize it's the beginning of the end of your job.

To restart, turn to page 86.
To end the stories and learn how to change your career, turn to page 119.

YOU ASK A QUESTION

You realize she has a good point. You ask her how she knew that. She tells you that she works with a lot of organizations. She explains how they're using technology to automate human tasks to save money.

You tell her it's not fair. She agrees. You ask her how she got into her current line of work. She explains her background. She tells you about her career change into user experience design. She tells you she was once in your situation. She chose user experience design because of the job security. She adds that she makes twice her previous salary.

You aren't sure what to say next.

If you ask to stay in contact, turn to page 100.
If you ask about the project she's working on, turn to page 101.
If you choose to end the conversation, turn to 103.

YOU STAY IN CONTACT

You ask the woman if you can talk to her another time to learn more about her experience. She agrees and shares her contact information. You don't know what you'll talk about.

After another month of pushing papers, you finally decide to follow up. You meet up to learn more. The conversation flows. She tells you about her experience making a career change. She tells you how she found an online program that taught her the skills to make change.

You learn you're not interested in user experience design. But you are inspired by her story. She offers to introduce you to another friend who works for a climate change organization. You're thrilled at the coincidence of the timing, as you just finished reading *The Uninhabitable Earth, Life After Warming*. You've been filled with despair after reading it, especially since you learned that by 2050 there will be more plastic than fish in the world's oceans. You've wondered how you can combine your work with fighting climate change.

You realize you need to act. You commit to learning more about the organizations working on climate change. You commit to upgrading your skills, as you've been on autopilot since you graduated college 10 years ago. You start exploring education opportunities that will help you make an impact in the climate change space. You don't know your next career move yet, but you're fired up to figure it out.

To restart, turn to page 86.

To end the stories and learn how to change your career, turn to page 119.

YOU ASK ABOUT THE PROJECT

You ask about the project she's working on. She tells you about working to make a better benefits app for your company. You tell her it sounds a million times more interesting than the projects you work on. You tell her you'd like to work on projects that have a big impact. She says she likes your attitude and invites you to apply for a job at her company. You do. And you get the job.

Two years later, you're killing it in your new position. Your coworkers are an enjoyable bunch and you make more money than you've ever made. While the job isn't perfect, there's no work-life balance, each day you're grateful for your job. You can't imagine what it'd be like if you had stayed in your last job.

For the past six months, you've managed the biggest project of your life. You've helped managers from three departments—Sales, Customer Service, and Marketing—to implement a predictive analytics software that increases your company's ability to target new customers. The software decreases the time it takes to find new customers, saving the company millions of dollars.

You head out to grab a coffee. At the coffee shop, you run into the Director of Operations. You say hello and introduce yourself. The Director tells you that they've heard good things about your work. She mentions that she's been impressed with your ability to work across departments and congratulates you on finishing your last big project. The Director wants you to join a meeting tomorrow but it's confidential. She asks that you not share the meeting information with others on your team, including your boss. You wonder if it's a promotion even though your boss isn't involved. You're not due for one but you certainly wouldn't say no.

You get back to your desk. You finally feel like you've made it. You're giddy about the future. A meeting invite from the Director of Operations pops up on your screen.

If you decline the meeting, turn to page 104.
If you accept the meeting, turn to page 106.

YOU END THE CONVERSATION

You end the conversation because it felt like a good stopping place. You continue to the meeting. On the way you pull out your phone, looking at online courses for user experience design. You don't see the giant hole in the middle of the hallway because you're walking while scrolling. You fall into the hole. You land face first, your hands crushed beneath your body, still clutching your phone. You break both of your hands.

You are unable to work for months. During the months off, you interact with Alexa to get things done. You start to wonder how Alexa works. You get more curious. One day, Alexa plays back a conversation it had recorded between you and a friend. You freak out. You take your Alexa to your garage and smash it.

You're spooked. You decide to start a new career in data privacy and artificial intelligence to fight against corporate surveillance.

To restart, turn to page 86.

To end the stories and learn how to change your career, turn to page 119.

YOU DECLINE THE MEETING

You hover over the accept button, insanely curious about this secret meeting. But you hit decline. You don't want more work. You don't want to have a discussion without your boss. Your boss has been an advocate for you in this job.

You hear nothing more about the secret meeting after declining. You mention the meeting invite with your boss. She says it's odd but says she doesn't know anything about it.

Six months later, you're called into your boss's office. She tells you that you're a great employee, the best she's ever had. She tells you it's been like family. Then she lays you off.

You're depressed. You changed careers so you would have more career security and now you're back at the start. You feel embarrassed.

You remember that there's no shame in being laid off. You start telling everyone what type of work you're looking for. You emphasize to everyone that you want to work for a company that actually values their employees.

As you start talking to more people about your interests, you learn about more opportunities. A friend of a friend tells you they work at a company that's developing a new approach to fighting food waste. You know nothing about food waste issues but you're curious because your friend tells you that everyone loves working there. You want to be part of something that's positive, so you start reading articles on food waste to learn more about the issue. You meet a food scientist at a party and end up talking about the issue. The more you learn, the more curious you become about the problem. You ask the food scientist how she got her job in that organization. She tells you her story and says she'll look out for any open jobs for you to join in the future.

You don't know which path you'll take but you start to feel better. There are options out there. You follow the possibilities.

To restart, turn to page 86.

To end the stories and learn how to change your career, turn to page 119.

YOU ACCEPT THE MEETING

You hit accept. You attend the meeting. You don't recognize half the people. You hear two people joking about whose MBA program is more superior. You learn they're consultants from a place called McKinsey. You feel out of place.

You quickly learn why you've been invited. The software project that you've led has created tremendous value for the company. In fact, it's so effective, they're going to lay off 65 percent of employees across three departments. The new software has eliminated the need for their jobs.

The company predicts they'll save $114 million a year in labor costs. You're shocked at the number but keep the feeling off your face. Nobody else seems shocked. In fact, as the consultants present their McKinsey-branded PowerPoint and point to their charts, they smile. They note that this was an expected result. It was part of the overall strategy to digitize the company.

You are the only one in the meeting who didn't know the outcome of your project.

The conversation turns to you. They congratulate you on leading the project that saved the company so much money. The Director of Operations turns to you to tell you the good news: you've been tapped to head a new department. They're consolidating all three departments into just one: Solutions. You're offered the job of Director of Solutions. Your people skills combined with your deep understanding of the software and AI technology is incredibly useful to the company. The promotion comes with a 40 percent raise. Everyone across the three departments will report to you, including your current boss.

You are shocked. You tell them you need more time to think. They push back. They note that this is a very sensitive subject. They'd like your commitment by the end of the day so they can move forward with the layoff plans. You don't ask what will happen to your current position if you don't accept.

If you choose to decline the position, turn to page 108.

If you choose to accept the position, turn to page 114.

YOU DECLINE THE POSITION

You decline the opportunity at the end of the meeting. Everyone is surprised. They thank you and remind you not to say a word to anyone else in the company about the layoffs.

You return to your desk. You look around at your colleagues. You like them and wonder how they'll navigate a layoff. You think of your coworker whose husband has cancer and needs the benefits. You think about new parents and how important it is to have stability at that time of their lives. You think about your coworkers who are above 55 and thought they'd retire at this company. Your mind races thinking about all the other people you've met over the past few months in other departments. They're all good employees. They work hard. None of that seems to matter.

You fall into a depressive funk. The thought of going back to work knowing so many people are about to get laid off makes you sick. You call in sick for the week.

During your time away, you think about what would happen if you told everyone. You wonder what kind of chaos it'd created if people knew ahead of time they were being laid off. What might they do? You play with the idea in your head.

If you decide to let people know, turn to page 109.
If you decide to keep the secret, turn to page 112.

YOU LET PEOPLE KNOW

You return to work after your time off. Your boss asks if you're okay. You lie and say yes.

You start your mission. You spend an hour telling the layoff news to the coworkers you trust most. You tell them the whole story. You name names. You tell them to tell three coworkers they trust. You create a massive game of telephone. You avoid digital communication so the security algorithms don't pick up on language on the flag list.

You notice people are staring at you more as the day goes on. Word is getting around. By lunch time, management gets wind of the telephone game. You get an email at the end of the day from the CEO:

> Subject: *Avoiding the Rumor Mill*
> *Hello everyone,*
> *It's come to our attention that there is talk of upcoming layoffs. We encourage everyone to take their concerns to their managers. We are committed to an open door policy.*
> *Remember, we consider you family here. Families don't air their dirty laundry. Avoid spreading unverified rumors. Your management team is committed to creating a place where you feel proud to come to work.*

You stand up. You head to the spot in your workplace with the most people and traffic. You climb on a desk. Eyes are on you. You are about to pull your best Jerry Maguire.

"Hello everyone!" you yell. You continue as loudly as possible, "By now you've heard the rumors that the company is planning to lay off 65 percent of employees from our three biggest departments. I'd like to confirm the rumors; they are true. I saw the numbers in a meeting last week. You've seen the two guys in suits over the past six months. They're consultants. They've been working with the leadership team on a plan to implement new automation systems that reduce the need for human jobs. I personally led the project that is going to put many of you out of work. For that, I want to apologize."

There are murmurs. You notice all the phones that are up and pointed at you. You take a deep breath and continue quickly. "Some of you will make the cut but most of you won't. It doesn't matter though: this place doesn't deserve your hard work. I'm leaving before they lay me off. I know not everyone can afford this—there's no shame in staying for your severance and unemployment.

"But for those who can afford it, I'm starting a new campaign to protect future employees from layoffs. It's called Humans First. And I want you to be part of it. I want to find a place to use your skills to build this new movement. I'm walking out of here right now and into a press conference. If you're pissed and want to let the world know, I invite you to join me."

You see security coming at you.

"So, who's coming with me?"

There are loud shouts but you can't hear them over the adrenaline.

Several people shout, "I'm out!" There is more commotion. Security escorts you out.

As you walk out the door, 75 employees follow you.

Your friend in PR has set up the press conference as part of your master plan. You announce a new campaign against the automation of jobs. You rally everyone behind the #humansnotbots movement. The people behind you cheer.

You set up a nonprofit organization called Humans First that advocates for labor and provides skill retraining programs. Your organization lifts up voices from communities that are at most risk from automation. You build, collaborate, and advocate. You don't know where this step is going to take you. But you know you have the power to shape the future of work and you're ready to shape it.

To restart, turn to page 86.

To end the stories and learn how to change your career, turn to page 119.

YOU KEEP THE SECRET

You keep the secret. It sucks. You put on a happy face for weeks at work but start to withdraw.

Then it hits. You're all rounded up in the largest conference room. They announce the news. Everyone in the room is being let go. The VP of Sales tells you that he thinks of you like family but, in order to do what's best for the family, they have to trim the fat. It's comical because nobody kicks out a family member to make more money.

People start crying but you are pissed. You pull up your phone during the Q&A session. You aren't locked out of your email just yet. With so many layoffs, IT hasn't gotten around to cutting everyone's access.

You hit reply all on the most recent all-employee email:

> *Three weeks ago, management offered me the job of Director of Solutions. I turned it down. Now I'm being laid off.*
> *Your loyalty and hard work do not matter here. Don't give your work ethic to a place that doesn't deserve it. Take your talents to a place that actually values you. Management is greedy as fuck. A pox on all their houses.*
> *Also, fuck this place.*

You bcc a friend who works in PR. You hit send. You return to your desk as the email hits inboxes. You hear the gasps and a few giggles. You pack up the few things on your desk as the murmurs grow. And then you hear a clap. And another. You look up to see everyone around you. You are being slow clapped as security surrounds you.

The slow clap turns to a fierce clap and chants of "Fuck this place! Fuck this place!" echo through the open office space. It's mad chaos and you don't even care as security escorts you out the door. One of them mouths *thank you* as you walk out. Your email goes viral and you end up on BuzzFeed, CNN, and all the rest of the interwebs because everyone feels the same.

You spend a month floating without a clue what to do. A friend drags you to an event about the impact of artificial intelligence on society. You only agree so you can get out of the house. At the event, you meet a woman who's a machine learning engineer. She recently quit an artificial intelligence startup because they'd asked her to develop a facial recognition product that was causing major harm to marginalized communities. You talk a lot about ethical AI and have an instant professional connection. Later, you start a company together. It's hard work. Together you build a product that predicts which Wall Street bankers are most likely to commit fraud. It takes months of building and testing but you land your first client: a major security firm. Your product is a huge success and you are making all the money.

You double down on your business to build a new product. This time, you build a product that predicts which CEOs are keeping money in offshore accounts and building sham companies to avoid taxes. Your product upsets the corporate power balance and you love it.

You don't know what the future holds but you're thrilled to be using your new skills to make all the money and create an impact.

To restart, turn to page 86.

To end the stories and learn how to change your career, turn to page 119.

YOU ACCEPT THE POSITION

You accept the offer. Your new salary allows you to pay off your student loans in four years instead of 10. You handle all layoffs as a result of the new software implementation. You didn't like it but understand how much it benefits the company's bottom line. You remind the soon-to-be ex-employees that your company is family and that you are only looking out for them.

Three months later, the VP of Operations tells you they're going to do another round of layoffs. A new automated system is now in place that eliminates 25 percent of positions in the accounting department. The company is making record profits but they want to ensure they're only investing in the right positions, and nothing more.

You're tasked with laying them off. Your boss tells you that if the layoffs go well without any repercussions, you'll get another raise.

If you decide to lay them off, turn to page 115.
If you decide not to lay them off, turn to page 117.

YOU LAY THEM OFF

You lay off another round of employees. It's not easy. The tears always get to you. You're human after all. You get so much praise from management that it makes it easier. You're so good at managing layoffs that the CEO has taken to calling you the Golden Hammer. You feel special and you're making more money than you've ever made.

At the end of the day, you get into your Tesla to drive home. You pull out of the parking lot. You try to take the left turn but the car immediately turns right. You grab the steering wheel but it's locked. The Tesla is on autopilot. You hear the doors lock. You see that all normal operating systems are frozen. You are cruising down the street at an "easy" 45 miles per hour.

You hear a voice from your speaker system: "Don't bother fighting it. Just sit back and enjoy the ride. We're all family here."

You freak out and try to call 911. The hacker has disabled your phone because it's connected to your car on Bluetooth.

You sit in your car, fearful you're being kidnapped. You yell at the car, demanding to know what's happening. You only get one answer. "We're family here. We are looking out for you." You ask more questions. You get the same response.

You arrive at a rally for the #humansnotbots campaign. You recognize the campaign from Instagram. You have a few friends who tagged their protest pictures with #humansnotbots.

Your Tesla parks and a group of former employees, three of whom were friends, surround your car. The Tesla unlocks. You jump out of the car. You see the group's smiling faces. You demand to know what's going on. They ask you to follow so they can show you. You don't feel threatened but you also don't feel like you have a choice.

You follow. You make your way through a crowd, listening to a speaker tell a story about losing their health insurance when they were laid off.

You're brought to a stage. You don't know what's about to happen. Your friend gestures to you to step up to the mic. She tells you to tell your story.

You are terrified.

All eyes are on you. You step up to the mic.

Your first words are: I'm sorry.

To restart, turn to page 86.

To end the stories and learn how to change your career, turn to page 119.

YOU DON'T LAY THEM OFF

You refuse to lay off any more people. You feel like a good person.

Your bosses are pissed. You're demoted and stripped of your title. You're now assigned to "special projects" but most of it is writing reports. Your new boss is an algorithm. You're moved out of your office and into a cubicle shared with a new coworker who eats tuna fish sandwiches at his desk daily.

You are now miserable. You start thinking it's time for a change. You've paid your student loans and built a bit of a savings account. You don't what you'll do but you know you can't stay put.

You're curious about a lot of things. You know there are possibilities.

To restart, turn to page 86.

To end the stories and learn how to change your career, turn to page 119.

PART THREE

How to Be an Agile Career-Changer

CHAPTER 5

Find Your Path

How to Change Careers

Reinventing your professional self can feel like a personal crisis. Many of us adopt our work as our identity. Our occupations become status symbols in conversations with others. Social gatherings are filled with conversations shaped by what we do: *I'm a designer. I'm an engineer. I'm a writer. I'm a firefighter.* The confidence in which others claim these identities makes anyone who isn't so sure about their professional identity feel like there is something wrong with them.

We define ourselves by occupation so when we decide to change it's more than changing our work. It's changing an identity. *If I change my work, who will I be?* It's tough to create a plan without an identity. After all, how do you change if you don't know who you'll be? Change without a plan creates more panic. This professional identity crisis keeps people stuck.

I can't blame you for feeling this way. American society doesn't give space to people in transition. We like tidy packages. Our social norms dictate that we should always have our shit together, striving toward success. That's at total odds with someone in a career transition.

Worse, society expects us to have our plan figured out at all times. We like confident certainty and problem solvers. Our social feeds are full of confident people talking about the decisions they made to get to the top. This makes people feel they can't move forward without The Plan.

Unfortunately, that's the opposite of how career development works. Exploration is the opposite of certainty. In coaching sessions, I've listened to executives who are still trying to figure themselves out despite being at the top of the corporate food chain. The intimacy of the coaching relationship means people share their professional insecurities and doubts. I learned very quickly that nearly everyone is uncertain about their future career path. Behind the scenes, everyone is always trying to sort it out.

You have the power to change the culture of professional pretending. The new economy has created a new professional normal. We're expected to keep our skills current, which often means a career change. We can't pretend our way through it. Career changes are learning experiences. They're messy because they're full of experimenting and ambiguity.

There's no reason to pretend. You don't have to have everything figured out before you make the first step. In fact, the first step in reinventing your professional self isn't making a plan. Your first step is to claim your space. Own the fact that you don't have everything figured out. Claim a space that says, "I'm in transition."

Let's play this out. Imagine you're at a social event with people you like (so not a networking event).

Friend 1:	So, what do you do?
Friend 2:	I'm in the middle of a career change.
Friend 1:	Oh, what are you going to be?
Friend 2:	I'm actually in transition right now. I'm trying to figure out what's next. It's a bit of a process but I'm learning.

When you claim your space, you control the narrative about your identity. You're not lost, you're exploring! You're not stuck, you're learning! Nobody is going to look down on you for that. In fact, some might be downright jealous. It takes gusto to make a career change. Openly claiming it and declaring your intent is powerful. American society expects tidy packages but they love a transformation story. In fact, I wonder why we don't have any career makeover shows.

This perspective shift is an essential starting point for career-changers. It gives you the space you need to move forward with a career change without knowing exactly what it is you want. If you already know what you want but aren't sure how to go about it, this act carves a space for you to move forward. Claiming your space puts you on a path. Notice, it doesn't give you The Plan. Instead, it gives you space to eventually shape The Plan. You don't need a plan to begin. You just need a path forward.

So, I want you to claim your space right now. Say these words out loud, wherever you are:

I'm going to make a change.

I don't care if you're reading this in public or around friends. Say it out loud.

I'll wait.

Okay, how did it feel? Probably a bit silly. Maybe a bit awkward because it probably looks like you're talking to yourself. But that's cool. Awkward is Change's best buddy, so expect Awkward to hang around as you go through your career change.

Embrace Awkward

The workplace and our employers are changing. That's forcing us to change. Change means getting comfortable with the unknown and getting comfortable with the unknown means learning and learning means discomfort and discomfort is awkward.

As a society, we're getting really good at avoiding discomfort. Algorithms serve up information that makes us feel good. We communicate in digital environments where can shape our responses and sentences into perfect quips. We avoid engaging with new people because conversations could be awkward. We avoid trying new things because we don't want to look dumb. Our social feeds are filled with people showing off success without messiness. We live in a culture that curates perfection and expects instant gratification.

The reality is that everyone's career is filled with mistakes and awkwardness. You've probably already made a cringe-worthy mistake in your career. If you haven't, you will. I may be the expert writing this book but I have enough awkward moments to fill a chapter. If you're having awkward moments, it's a sign that you're learning.

Make peace with mistakes as you move forward. Embrace Awkward. Don't fight it. Don't run from it. Stare at it, examine it, learn from it, and move on. Remember, the feeling of awkwardness is short term. It won't last. If you take the time to reflect on it, you'll learn something too. Sometimes those mistakes make for great stories to laugh at later. Embracing awkward moments will remind you that we're not perfect people walking around all the time. We've all carrying around buckets of awkwardness.

It's time to make a step forward in your career change. So, let's start the process.

Choose Your Career Change Path

Many of you are at different places in your career change. I want to make it easy for you to get the information you need no matter what career transition stage you are in. I wish I had a magical sorting hat to get you to the right part of the book, but I don't. So, I need you to do your best to sort yourself.

If you haven't figured out what your next career move is, you're an **Explorer**. The explorer section includes a lot of exploratory exercises and encouragement to help you identify your next career jump.

If you know your next career step but need guidance on how to upskill, you're a **Learner**. The learner section breaks down how to reverse engineer the upskill process, set realistic expectations, and identify learning experiences that will help you build new skills and support your career transition. The explorer section will lead into the learner section but the learner section will not lead into the explorer section.

If, after reading to this, you decide you're just up for a job change, you're a **Searcher**. The searcher section shows you how to leave your job and find a better one. The explorer and learner section will lead into the searcher section.

*All **Explorers** turn to page 127.*
*All **Learners** turn to page 167.*
*All **Searchers** turn to page 215.*

CHAPTER 6

Exploring

Unleash Your Curiosity

Leonardo da Vinci had a to-do list. It wasn't any normal to-do list, obviously, because he's Leonardo fucking da Vinci. Leo kept a big list of all the things he'd like to learn and people he'd like to talk to. According to author and historian Toby Lester, who wrote *Da Vinci's Ghost: Genius, Obsession, and How Leonardo Created the World in His Own Image*, Leonardo da Vinci was a persistent observer and notetaker. Inside Leo's famous notebooks filled with sketches, the author found a to-do list from 1490. NPR had the lists translated in 2011.[38] Here's what he wanted to learn in the 15th century:

- Get the master of Arithmetic to show you how to square a triangle
- Draw Milan

---

[38]NPR, "Leonardo's To-Do List."

- Discover the measurement of the Castello (The Duke's Palace itself)
- Ask Maestro Antonio how mortars are positioned on bastions by day or night
- Find a master of hydraulics and get him to tell you how to repair a lock, canal, and mill in the Lombard manner

Leo's list was more than a to-do list. It was a curiosity list. His quest for knowledge was so insatiable, he couldn't keep it all in his head. He's been described as a person of "unquenchable curiosity."[39] This perfectly captures the essence of Leo. And, quite conveniently, it captures exactly how I want you to think during the exploration phase of your career change.

In the exploration phase, I want you to be like Leo. I want you to grab hold of your curiosity and look at your everyday life through the lens of opportunity. What can you learn? Who can you talk to? Where should you go?

The exploration phase of your career transition is full of thrills. You're going to talk to people and investigate organizations. You get to explore on the sly at work, channeling any frustration you might have about your job into glorious exploration. This phase is relatively leisurely. You don't need a résumé to do it. You only need an unquenchable curiosity and a willingness to indulge it.

---

[39] PBS, "Mona Lisa."

EXERCISE: Be Like Leo

Leonardo da Vinci kept a notebook where he wrote down everything that struck his curiosity. As a career explorer, I want you to get into the habit of doing the same. First, get a notebook. You're going to meet a lot of people in this journey and do some research too. Your curiosity needs a landing place and your thoughts need a home.

Avoid taking notes on your phone, where you can easily get distracted. Instead, write them down with pen and paper. You are more likely to remember things when you write them down, as opposed to typing them.

Now, start the exploration stage with a curiosity exercise. Spend a week noting down all the things you're curious about. Every time you start to wonder about something or someone, write it down. The goal is to find things that you're curious about and capture them. Take time to note your curiosities, no matter how big or small.

Use these questions as a guide:

- *What would you like to learn?*
- *What do you want to know about?*
- *Who would you like to meet?*

This exercise is designed to build your curiosity muscles. If you decide you're curious about having a conversation with the CEO of your company, write it down. Maybe you want to learn how to draw animals or you want to understand how CSS works.

After a week, set aside 30 minutes to review your list. Reflect on your answers. Reflection is where the learning magic happens. Pay attention to the things on your list that make you excited. What items and themes stand out?

Now, pick one thing from the list to do. Commit to it and give yourself a reasonable deadline. Don't forget to reward yourself when you accomplish it.

This exercise neatly mirrors the process of a career change. Career exploration is about noticing what interests you professionally, reflecting on your options, and committing to one of them.

Set Ridiculous Goals

When I'm 65 I want to open my own sauna and hot tub place. I already love to soak my bones at saunas and in hot tubs. At 65, I'm going to want to soak my weary-ass bones all the damn time, so I want to open my own place. I'm going to invite all my old-ass friends to soak their weary bones too. We'll soak our naked, wrinkly bodies while smoking and giggling our evening away. We'll be warm and I'll make some good money because, let's be real, our generation isn't retiring on some pension at 65. If I'm going to have to work my bones into my seventies or eighties, my bones—and the bones of all my friends—are gonna need a hell of a lot more TLC.

This is a ridiculous career goal. When I tell my very support-ive partner, she shakes her head with a knowing smile that says, "Yes, but when will your career pay off your student loans?" She's incredibly patient with me now. But I know she'll want to soak those old bones too.

I'm a bit obsessed with this bone soaking place. I've got 20 years to figure it out. I may just end up sampling a bunch of soaking pools and saunas over the next 20 years under the guise of market research. But that's perfectly okay. The point of having ridiculous career goals is to imagine the possibilities.

Ridiculous goals are a lot of fun. Setting ridiculous goals also opens up the possibility for multiple paths. It gives you the space to define your needs and wants and the time in which you want to achieve these goals. Ridiculous goals don't have to happen right away.

Exploration is the best phase of your career change. It requires no commitment to anyone but yourself. You don't have to have a résumé to do it or even quit your job. You simply need to follow your curiosity.

Setting ridiculous goals trains your brain to be okay with ambiguity. It allows you to be creative with your future and imagine a world with multiple possibilities. It gives you permission to dream.

Setting ridiculous goals is not an exercise in career planning. That's why it's such a good exercise for career-changers. This is not the time to make a career plan. Instead, I want you to think of this time as career pathing. Once you decide on a path, you can make a plan. But until you've identified that path, you can't plan.

Creating career paths instead of plans gives you permission to change your mind. I've met so many people who stay in careers because they feel they can't change their mind. They feel they've committed to a career plan and have to stick with it. It's a common feeling among those who come from families with certain expectations or those who invested thousands of dollars in a degree that they're still paying off. They feel an obligation to The Plan.

So, let's kick off your exploration process by setting some ridiculous goals. I want you to write down everything that you'd like to do as a career. Make them as big as possible. Make them audacious. Be bold. Create ridiculous goals that are so far-fetched you're pretty sure they will never happen. That's perfectly fine.

This is a warm-up. Just like you need to stretch before you work out, you need to imagine the possibilities before you get down to the actual goals. You don't have to commit to your ridiculous goals. You'll get to actual, realistic, concrete goals later in this chapter. Finding your next career step starts with flexibility of the mind and ridiculous paths.

Carve Your Path

In the exploration phase anything is possible. This is your time to explore all the different opportunities and paths that interest you. The goal of the exploration process is to finish three sentences:

- I want to transition into a job where I *(define type of work)*.
- I want to work for a company that *(describe type of company)*.
- I'm interested in working in an industry that *(describe the industry that interests you)*.

Getting to this goal requires equal parts research and self-reflection. To find your next career move, you need to complete four actions:

- Reflect on your career needs
- Explore companies that appeal to you
- Survey the landscape of opportunities
- Gather new perspectives from people

Self-reflection creates space for you to define your career needs and goals. Exploring companies helps you identify industries and companies you belong in. Surveying the landscape of opportunities helps identify jobs that put you on your next career path. Gathering new perspectives from people gives you advice and insights that shape your next career path, while also building valuable communication skills.

The following sections break down each of these actions and include exercises to help you complete the actions. Each exercise is designed to make you to reflect on your learnings and choices. In our busy work lives, we rarely take time to step back and ask ourselves what we actually need in a career. The exploration process is the ideal time to do this. Working through the exercises gives you space and time to carve your path.

I want you to build and use new skills as you go through the career transition process. Learning to collect qualitative data, identify themes, engage with people, and pull all the pieces together is a useful skill that you will continue to use in the workplace. I want you to flex these mental muscles and learn something new as you identify a new career path.

Assessments are a common tool for career-changers in the exploration phase. I have left out any recommendations for online assessments from this section because they don't help you build skills. Assessments have their place in the career change process. If you're the type of person who likes an online test to figure out your strengths and personality, by all means, take them. Then come back to these exercises. In the end, you're going to pull together all the data from the exploration phase to help you take a step forward toward your new career.

Get a deadline

There are three stages to a career transition: Exploring, Learning, and Searching. To find your deadline, divide your career transition process into thirds. One third for exploring career path possibilities, another third for learning new skills, and the last third for the job search.

The time you take to explore all the career path possibilities is up to you. You set the pace. But you need a deadline to motivate you. Without a deadline, you risk getting stuck in exploration forever. You want to move forward, not swim around in circles.

Your deadline is based on when you want to start that shiny new career. Visualize yourself in a new career, making all the money, feeling fresh. When do you want this to happen? What will you need in order to quit your current job? Do you have enough financial resources to support you in that pursuit?

Pick a date or month to start your new career and set your deadline. Now work backward from that date. If you want to start a new career in a year, you could budget four months for exploration. This deadline is semi-flexible. You can change it if life circumstances happen or you discover new information that changes your path. For example, if you discover during your learning experience research that you're going to need six months to learn how to become a data scientist, and you only budgeted for three months, then you'll need to readjust your deadline.

It is important to be true to your deadline in order to level up in your career. Deadlines force us to make progress. For procrastinators, a deadline is the only thing that will save us. Make a commitment to your future self right now by setting a deadline. Your future self will thank you for the hard work.

Slay your sloth

I have an inner sloth. It eats weed brownies and has a grumpy disposition. It doesn't want to wake up to write this book every morning. It whispers to me through a stoney haze every time I get stuck, and says, "Hey, why work so hard, come get stoned and watch Netflix." I slay it every day and every day it comes back grumpy as hell. (Obvi, my inner sloth regenerates.) Some days it wins and I don't write. Most days, I slay my sloth.

Your inner sloth isn't a cute little lazy animal. It's a beast. The word *sloth* actually means "a reluctance to work or make effort." Everyone has a beastly inner sloth.

Career changes are a lot of work. They take effort and persistence at each step. Your inner sloth hates work, especially more work on top of everyday work. So, you must slay your inner sloth on the regular. There will be days when you fail to slay it, and it wins. The regenerative sloth is a strong, persistent beast. But that's okay. We all need rest days. It's okay to hang with your sloth for a day or two. Just don't get too comfortable. You can't hang with your inner sloth every day and expect to make progress.

If slaying your metaphorical sloth makes you uncomfortable, kick or gently place your inner sloth outside so it can't bother you for the day. You got shit to do. You need your motivation.

Don't let your inner sloth slow your momentum.

Reflect on Your Professional Self

Every company has an About page. Each job description comes with an overview of the company. There is a reason for this: companies are communicating to you who they are in hopes that you'll be a match. In order to find your next career, you need to know what you want. You must identify the values, needs, likes, and skills that shape your professional self. From there, you'll be in a better position to find career paths that match.

When you're struggling in your career it's easy to lose sight of what you need from a career. Check in with your professional self to understand your career needs.

Start with the big question: Why do you want to change careers? You already know you want to make the jump. Naming the reason brings your motivation into the open, ensuring it doesn't slip away when things get tough. It's also powerful to see our reasons reflected back at us. Sometimes it's as simple as *I want to be paid what I'm worth and feel valued* or *I want to have an impact.* Other times it's more complicated. *I'm noticing that younger people have skills I don't have* or *I want to be more agile in my career so I can always provide for my family.*

Then reflect on your past experience to understand the type of work that motivates you. What excites you about your work? What bores you?

Finally, reflect on what you want out of your next career. Think about outcomes. What do you want from your career change? What do you expect to happen when you change careers?

Be honest with yourself. It's common for people to assume a new job or career is the ultimate problem solver. You might think a $40,000 raise will solve all your problems. And it might. But it might also create new ones. You might choose a new career path where you are expected to be on at all hours of the day, responding to emails or a micromanaging boss. Or you might find a new career that has better life balance but fewer perks than your current career. There are trade-offs in all changes.

The two reflection exercises on the next pages will help you go deeper to understand your professional interests and needs. They are questions that I frequently use in coaching sessions to help people check in with their professional selves. Normally, these questions are spread over several coaching sessions. So, take your time answering them. There's no pressure to answer them in one sitting. This is your time to check in with your professional self.

EXERCISE: Your Professional Self

When you're investing the time to make a career jump, make sure the new career path works for your current lifestyle, not someone else's. Defining your needs, values, likes, and skills helps you ensure the next career jump is a match for you.

The questions below help you check in with your professional self. If it's been a while, it may take time to answer them.

Values
What does good work mean to you?
What type of company do you want to work for?
How do you want to feel at the end of a day?
What kind of impact do you want to make in your work?

Needs
What do you need to feel valued at your workplace?
How much do you need to make to pay your bills?
How much do you need to live comfortably?
What benefits do you need to fit your lifestyle?

Likes
What type of work do you enjoy?
What kind of people do you like to work with?
What type of boss do you like?
How would you like your boss to make you feel?

Skills
What are you good at?
What aren't you good at?
What skills would you like to use in your next job?
What would you like to learn how to do?

EXERCISE: Your Top Five

Changing careers is an act of improving your professional life. You define what improvement means to you.

Below is a list of career wants. These are common characteristics that people seek in a new career. Rank them in order of importance to you with 1 being the most important.

The last two items are fill in the blank. Use them to define anything you don't see on this list.

___ I want to make a good salary

___ I want good health benefits

___ I want a lot of vacation

___ I want a flexible work schedule

___ I want a boss who values me

___ I want to have time with my family/friends/hobbies outside of work

___ I want to feel valued in my work

___ I want a company that invests in my professional development

___ I want a role where I can work on interesting projects

___ I want to make an impact with my work

___ I want to move up in the company fast

___ I want a leadership role

___ I want to learn new skills

___ I want a company whose values match mine

___ I want _____

___ I want _____

After ranking them, write down your top five. Then transfer the top five to a place where you will see them regularly.

These are your career metrics. You'll use them throughout your career transition to evaluate new paths and jobs and even negotiate when you've got a new job offer. Even better, you can return to this list after you've settled into a new career to see how your priorities shift.

Of course, you'll likely get more out of your next career than just five things. Ranking them sets your priorities straight from the start of the exploration process.

Fall in Love with Companies

Today I fell head over heels in love with a company. I'm a happily employed woman with plenty going on. But the minute I locked eyes on this company, I was ready to throw it all away for a chance to be with this company. They're hot, fun, and they seem to really care.

The company is Glitch. They describe themselves as "the friendly community where everyone can discover and create the best stuff on the web." One look at their company website and you know you're looking at a creative company. When I clicked on their Careers page I swooned.

This is a company that's hitting all the marks. First, they offer 20 days a year of vacation. Their health insurance is 100 percent paid, plus unlimited sick days. They even point out that it's okay to take time off to care for a sick loved one. They write, "We don't think you should have to use vacation time for these unexpected circumstances."

I'm melting. When's the last time you saw a company acknowledge the fact that our loved ones get sick? They also offer a "learning and development" budget of $3,500 and tuition reimbursement. Companies like this understand that the future belongs to the learners. A company that provides a learning budget is a company that cares about its employees.

But it gets better. Their career page explains why working at Glitch is different. They commit to "no endless meetings," describing a working environment that strives to have fewer meetings. When meetings happen, they keep to an agenda. They go further:

> *"Each person on the team takes turns keeping notes*
> *because we don't want women or other underrepresented*

*team members to feel unduly obligated to handle such
tasks, and every meeting with more than 2 people has
notes shared to the entire company so that everyone
knows what's going on."*[40]

Hot damn. Glitch also prides itself on very few email mes-
sages, noting that employees receive fewer than a dozen emails in
a week from coworkers.

I can't imagine that in any of my previous places of work.
The list of things goes on, from noting their 100 percent paid
healthcare to a commitment to inclusion that's not just fluff. They
admit they used to be quite homogeneous but that they "screwed
up and we're not making any excuses for it." They're actively
building an inclusive culture, starting from the top. Marry me.

On top of it all is a commitment to transparency. They make
their employee handbook public.

Glitch's work style, transparency, and commitment to inclusion resonate with me. These are my values. These are what matter to me. If I'm going to apply my skills and talent and work
ethic to a place, I want it to be somewhere like this.

Companies like Glitch represent the future. They give hope
that some companies still value their employees. The future of
work is filled with companies that are rewriting the rules of
work. For every old-school company that refuses to invest in
their employees or clings to traditional 9 to 5 workplace rules,
there are companies transforming their cultures and bucking the
trend of doing the bare minimum for their employees.

We hear a lot about startups that offer perks like free food.
While I'm on Team Food any day, the workplace needs to offer

[40]Glitch, "Careers."

more than just free food. Each company has a culture that shapes your experience on the job. These cultures offer different management and work styles. For example, Automattic, the company that runs WordPress, is a fully remote company. Everyone, from the admins to the executives, works from a location of their choice. Each year, the company flies everyone to a new location in the world to meet up. Dreamy.

Other companies offer flexible scheduling, meaning you don't have to show up between the hours of 9 to 5, making it easier for parents to navigate their kids' schedules. Some companies are starting to include daycare as part of their benefits, while others offer student loan contributions. Some organizations just do good work and it feels good to do work with a purpose. There is so much more to the world of work than what's directly in front of us, day to day.

We spend 40 hours or more a week at our places of work. They're basically our second home. As we take control of our careers and create our own paths, we have the power to define what we need from companies. It's similar to defining what we want in a partner and our dream home. You wouldn't go house shopping without a clear idea of what you want in your living space. The same goes for your career. I want you to fall in love with organizations that make your heart sing.

Find your match

Glitch makes my heart swoon. I want you to find the companies that make your heart swoon. I want you to imagine your ideal place of work. What does it look like? What does it feel like? What are the people like? Exploring new companies at this stage of your career transition gives you the freedom to find the places of work that fit your ideal.

With millions of companies, it's hard to know where to start exploring. Focusing on an industry is an ideal way to discover companies. An industry is a collection of companies whose products or services are related. Common examples you've likely heard of in passing are the tourist industry, tech industry, and film industry. Each organization that you've worked for maps to an industry. For example, if you work as a program manager at a university, you're working in the higher education industry. Within industries, there are also smaller classifications. So, if you worked as a program manager in a study abroad office, you'd also work in the international education industry.

Industries are useful categories for career exploration. Career changes usually involve a jump from one industry into another. If you are working as a program manager in higher education but are curious about becoming a designer in the VR space, start by exploring the VR industry. VR is part of the tech industry, but also a niche within the tech industry. As you explore the VR industry, you'll quickly find that it's often tied in with Augmented Reality (AR). Expect to explore opportunities in both niches.

Start exploring industries as a way to discover new companies and career paths. We are living in a golden age of content. There are industry newsletters, podcasts, YouTube series, meet ups, Facebook groups, and so much more. People are creating and connecting around shared professional interests. Find your potential career path by diving into all of this content. If VR interests you, sign up for newsletters so you get information delivered to your inbox daily. Commit to opening one email daily to learn about companies and understand the industry vocabulary. Learn what's important to people in this industry. Some newsletters even list open jobs. Read the jobs and familiarize yourself with the job titles and requirements to explore if they're a fit for you.

Try out podcasts and YouTube videos. Commit to one podcast a week from an industry source. Try a podcast like the Real Virtual Show, to hear perspectives from industry leaders. Watch YouTube videos about AR/VR to learn about the products and understand the diverse use cases.

As you explore the industry, take notes on what you learn. Write down the names of companies you learn about. Then look them up. Explore their About pages and social media to learn about their culture.

As you immerse yourself in their worlds, you'll discover ideas, paths, and opportunities. This exploration process builds your knowledge management skills. Your ability to find resources and evaluate their usefulness is an in-demand skill in the workplace.

EXERCISE: Company Love

There's no Tinder for companies (yet). So, get your Google fingers ready, it's time to become a researcher. You're going to dive deep into industries and work cultures. So, let's investigate your options.

First, select a target industry. If you don't have a target industry, check out Wikipedia. They have a surprisingly robust list of industries to explore in their section titled "Outline of Industry."

Then go nuts collecting content. Sign up for newsletters. Download podcasts. Find YouTube channels. Spend a couple weeks consuming this content. Write down companies that you hear about on your curiosity list. You don't have to recognize the company names. Just write them down.

Once you get 15 companies on your curiosity list, dive deeper into the companies. Write down the answers to the questions below:

- What can you learn from their website?
- What can you learn from their social media feeds?
- What can you learn from articles about them?

When you've finished diving into the companies, you'll have a better idea of which companies fit your career interests.

Once you understand the companies, match a company to the question below. A company can match to more than one question. In fact, if you find a company that matches to most of these questions, that's a good sign that you've found a company you can crush on. Keep any company that you are crushing on as a model of where you'd like to work. You'll need these examples when you start the job search.

- Which company do you think would treat you the best?
- Which company has the best benefits?
- Which company inspires you?
- Which company's values match yours?
- Which company has people like you on their leadership teams?
- Which company's products or services interest you the most?
- Which company would you most like to work for?

Survey the Landscape of Opportunities

In a previous career I was a study abroad advisor for a university. When I told people what I did, they assumed my job consisted of traveling around the world visiting students and exchange partners. I had to tell them I didn't actually do that. Instead, I spent most of my time in Seattle answering emails and sitting in meetings. It was a cool job but it was a hell of a lot less glamorous than people thought.

It's common to make assumptions about people's work. If you've heard a job title enough times, it's easy to think you understand what the work involves. A good friend of mine is a firefighter. Once she told me that firefighting is a lot like customer service. She deals with all types of people with a range of needs. She's responsible for listening to their needs and acting accordingly to solve the issue at hand. I had never thought about firefighting in that way. I incorrectly assumed they just fought big blazes and saved cats from trees.

To find a path for your next career, look beyond titles to understand job abilities. Job abilities are the collection of skills, expertise, and talents that are expected in any given role. Instead of assuming what a person *does* in a job, learn what a person *should be able to do* in a job.

For example, a lot of people make assumptions about travel writers. They assume a travel writer just writes about fancy places. However, that's not the case. A travel writer should be able to do a lot more than just write about fancy places. An aspiring travel writer should be able to:

- interview travelers and locals about their experiences
- collaborate with digital designers

- analyze social media and Google analytics
- write clever copy for newsletters and photo captions
- write engaging stories in long form for print and digital
- design with HTML and CSS
- use a content management system
- edit before the formal editing process
- seek out new story angles to tell in familiar places
- troubleshoot challenging travel logistics
- understand marketing automation
- have a basic understanding of video
- listen to customer needs
- work within a limited budget
- collaborate with brand partners

That's obviously a lot more than just writing. As a career-changer, you need to get to know jobs beyond the titles and assumptions.

Now think about your current job. What should someone in your job *be able to do?* Someone is going to want your current job in the future. So, do them a favor now and write down all the things they *should be able to do* in your job. It's a good exercise to get you in the habit of understanding job abilities and getting beyond job titles.

A landscape of opportunities

The best advice I ever received on how to change careers came from a coworker. She told me to get into the habit of reading job descriptions. Not scanning. Reading. It's been my secret weapon for every career change.

When you read job descriptions regularly, you understand the landscape of opportunities. Each time I needed to exit a mediocre job, I'd start by reading job descriptions. Each day I'd spend 20 minutes looking at all kinds of jobs, whether I was qualified for them or not. I'd categorize them as interesting or not interesting, and possible or not possible. This habit became the foundation for all my career changes.

Reading job descriptions is not the most exciting way to pass 20 minutes. As a career-changer, however, the habit of reading job descriptions invites you to consider the opportunities. Each job post is a company showing you a possible path. They basically ask you, "Do you like this? Can you do this?"

Once you see the landscape of opportunities, you're able to evaluate whether or not the opportunities in front of you are even a possibility. For example, if you read jobs for a week and learn that your experience matches really well with public policy jobs but working in public policy puts you to sleep, you know that those jobs are not a possibility. Feel free to ignore them as you go forward. Knowing what's not a fit for you is just as valuable as learning what is a fit. Finding a career that excites you is often a process of elimination.

There are all kinds of work for all kinds of people. I know I'll never be excited by a career in financial analysis. Yet, one of my good friends oversees the budget for her entire organization. Powerful people rely on her analysis and insights from her work on the budget. She's the all-seeing eye in her organization, which in turn gives her a lot of power where she works. I could never do it. I'm glad I know that. I can happily ignore all the budget-related job postings for the rest of my life.

How to read job descriptions

If job descriptions were written better, they'd all start with "here's what you should be able to do." But they're not. They're a mess. That's why we scan them looking for matches like education and years of experience. It's easier to match our backgrounds to those qualities.

To figure out your next career, learn how to read job descriptions and translate them into their job abilities. This makes it easier to evaluate if you could do that type of work.

For example, here's an example of a community manager job posting at a film company that uses storytelling to impact society in a positive way. These are the responsibilities and requirements:

Responsibilities

- Be our main community point of contact across social media, email, and blog, ensuring that members are heard, valued, and always have a positive interaction with us
- Help to run our Instagram channel by implementing the already developed strategy, posting daily content, and looking at how to develop our strategy to grow our audience
- Run our email support through Help Scout, which is one of our main ways of supporting our community. While some of this is rather mundane, the majority is an opportunity for real connection with members and to surprise and delight them

- Help to write community emails (to our 30K email list), publish blog posts, and develop content for the community (supporting a YouTube series around storytelling, as an example)

Requirements

- Possess a strong sense of leadership and ownership
- Experience with social media, especially Instagram
- Ability to learn and adapt to new technology quickly
- Advanced writing skills and proofing skills
- Must be extremely detail oriented
- Design in Canva or Photoshop is a plus, but not mandatory

Now, let's translate that into job abilities. A community manager should be able to:

- communicate authentically with community members on email and Instagram
- find creative ways to grow Instagram outreach while maintaining existing strategy
- tell stories across multiple platforms (email, Instagram, blog, YouTube)
- lead with positive intention
- explore new technology comfortably

Now it's a lot easier to evaluate this job. You can ask yourself: is this the type of work that I'd like? Is this the type of work that I could do? If your answer is yes to both of those questions, it's a possible career path for you. If not, you know that this work isn't a match.

Job postings are how companies show you the types of work that are possible. As a career-changer, use this information to guide you. Start paying attention to all types of work by reading job descriptions regularly. As you read, don't focus on whether or not you can do the job listed. Instead, categorize jobs into work you *would like to do* and work you *could learn* to do. When you spend time reading job postings, you'll see a new world of possibilities and career paths.

EXERCISE: Read All the Jobs

It's time to explore your job possibilities by reading job descriptions. Start the process by setting up saved job search alerts. Every job search platform offers the option to save your job searches and get an email delivered weekly with a roundup of jobs that interest you.

Pick a few keywords from the industry that you'd like to work in. For example, if you're interested in working in VR/AR, search on Indeed or LinkedIn for jobs with those keywords. Explore the filters to find roles that interest you. Then save the search. Each week, an email roundup of VR/AR jobs will arrive in your inbox. It's likely there will be tons of jobs. As you start to understand the landscape of opportunities, use the filters to narrow down your job interests by job function, location, and experience level.

Each week, pick three jobs to read. Read through each post. Then ask yourself two clarifying questions:

- Does this type of work interest me?
- Could I do this job?

If you answer yes to both of those questions, write down the job's title and a short sentence that summarizes the job. Note any vocabulary or technical skills that are foreign to you. Do not worry whether you are qualified yet. That part comes much later.

Repeat this exercise until you have 30 possible jobs on your list. The goal of this exercise is to build a list of job possibilities. As you explore jobs, you will learn new career paths, identify new skills to learn, and discover new companies.

Seek Out New Perspectives

I'm on my fourth career change and currently contracting as an AI chatbot designer. When people ask what I do, I get three types of responses. The first answer is, "Interesting!" followed by a change in subject. They aren't quite sure how to respond because my job doesn't fit neatly into a category. The second response is to ask what a chatbot designer actually does (I make chatbots sound more human, I tell them). The third is a question, "How did you get into that job?" This is my favorite question.

This is what I tell them: I'm obsessed with artificial intelligence but I don't have a technical background. I read everything I can about AI in the workplace. At some point I learned that some companies use interview chatbots as part of the hiring process. So, I started testing them out, seeing how well they worked. I wrote about conversational experiences with chatbots on my blog. One day, I noticed a company that makes chatbots had a job opening for a conversational designer. I didn't know that job existed. I didn't exactly qualify but I also didn't not qualify. I can write, I love language, I understand user experience and design principles, and I have a basic knowledge of AI and machine learning, though I don't code very much. I applied and put a link to my blog post in my cover letter. I got the job.

In the career-change process, stories like these show you what's possible. New perspectives help you shape your career transition and bring those job descriptions to life. They also help you build important professional relationships in the process.

How to have curious conversations

"Human relationships are rich and they're messy and they're demand-ing. And we clean them up with technology. We sacrifice conversation for mere connection." —Sherry Turkle[41]

We are surrounded by people with stories. As a career-changer, you need to hear stories about real professional expe-riences. Stories bring career change possibilities to life. Seeing yourself in the stories of others fires you up. People will tell you how all these skills, companies, and hard life decisions play out. It's not hard to get people to talk. People like talking about themselves. In your exploration quest, start asking curious questions.

The most powerful question a career-changer can ask a person is, "How did you get into that?" It works best with the follow-up power question, "How did you know that's what you wanted to do?" It's one thing to consider a new career path, but quite another to know if it's what you actually want to do. Hearing people share their experiences about how they knew for certain they wanted to go down a career path is a powerful expe-rience. Talk to enough people and you'll see yourself in those experiences and find clarity in them. Engaging with people also makes you a better listener, a skill that's in high demand, yet low supply in the workplace.

Seek out people with interesting careers and ask curious questions. We all need inspiration during a career change. People are carrying around micro-doses of inspiration. Your goal is to seek out those doses.

---

[41]TED Blog, "Sherry Turkle."

As a career-changer, conversations are one of the most useful tools in the exploration process, second only to research. Curious conversations take you to unexpected places in your exploration process. They can lead to new jobs, mentorship, and support. Yet people are increasingly struggling with in-person conversation.

Conversations without technology as the medium are increasingly difficult for most people. We live in an era where we spend more time communicating in digital environments than face-to-face conversations. We are efficient in our texts, generous with our likes, and wicked with our GIFs. We type our way through the workday using text, email, and Slack. We exercise our fingers, not our voice. The result is that people are feeling more anxious than ever about face-to-face conversations. When people get anxious, they start avoiding conversations.

The psychologist and researcher, Dr. Sherry Turkle, examined our reluctance toward face-to-face conversation in her outstanding book, *Reclaiming Conversation: The Power of Talk in a Digital Age*. Through hundreds of interviews with students, professionals, and families, she holds up a mirror to our phone-obsessed culture and the effect it's having on our ability to have face-to-face conversations.

She notes that our "flight from conversation undermines our relationships, creativity, and productivity."[42] While her book is full of insights, I was struck by her observations that people struggle to have conversations because they're not scripted. With so much time spent in controlled digital spaces, where you can craft a message perfectly before sending, people are intimidated by unstructured, open-ended conversations. The result is that many people

---

[42]MIT, "Sherry Turkle."

are avoiding conversation altogether due to anxiety about saying the wrong thing.

Finding a new career path requires a commitment to curious conversations. Curious conversations are discussions with the intent to learn something new. These conversations aren't talking for the sake of talking. They're purposeful. Instead of asking people what they do, ask curious questions: How did you get into that? How did you know that you wanted to do that?

Curious conversations are about opportunism. You get to decide who interests you. You don't need to show up at boring networking events to have curious conversations. Find interesting people in your life, at work, and other places where you spend your time. Start conversations with them. If there's someone at your current job who has a job that interests you, go talk to them about it. Create an opportunity to engage with them. Take what you learn from that conversation and apply it to your own career choices. Maybe you learn that you'd never want to do their job. Maybe you learn that you could do their job because it turns out you have a similar background. Or maybe you learn they have a job you didn't know exists. Conversations are full of potential.

If you're the type of person who shies away from conversations, it's time to learn how to have curious conversations.

First, get your mindset right. Open yourself up to the idea of talking to new people, regardless of how it might go. Embrace the awkwardness of it. Don't let the fear of the unknown or mistakes stop you from engaging with people.

Next, get a conversational strategy. A strategy is a reflection of what you'd like to learn, not a plan. Ask yourself: What do I want to learn about this person? What do I want to know? What do I want them to know about me?

Then get a framework.

1. Share your career transition story
2. Use the curious questions combo
3. Embrace awkward and focus on flow
4. Deploy an exit sentence

In practice, curious conversations look like this. Start with the introduction story. Tell people you're interested in learning about their career path. If you're talking to a person outside of your workplace, tell them you're changing careers: "Hey, you might not know this, but I'm in the middle of a career change. I'm not sure what I'm going to do next but I'm really curious about your job."

Next, hit them with the curious questions combo, starting with, "How did you get into your field of work?" Then follow up with, "How did you know you wanted to do that kind of work?"

Now let the conversation flow. Conversational ability requires you to adapt to whatever words a person throws at you. Add your thoughts. Ask follow-up questions. Make eye contact. Let the conversation exist. Embrace the awkwardness.

When you're out of conversation or time, end it with an exit sentence. Exit sentences help you wrap up a conversation without waiting for the conversation to die out. Try this exit sentence: "Thanks so much for sharing your experience with me. It's been helpful. Let's stay in touch." Exchange social details to stay in touch, or not. And then say good day and move along. Exit sentences are important because some conversations will be boring as hell. Not all curious conversations are winners. Exit sentences help you end a conversation in a polite, tidy manner.

Building your conversational ability is like going to the gym. You have to commit to it. There will be days where you don't want to do it. That's fine. You don't have to go to the gym every day. But to see results in your career change you have to commit. Hit the conversation gym on a regular basis during your exploration phase. You'll surprise yourself at how good you get at navigating different people and conversational situations. You'll build an important Power Skill for the workplace. But best of all, you'll get motivation and perspective to help you find your way in this exploration phase.

EXERCISE: 50 Conversations

Face-to-face conversations are essential for career-changers. Just reading about a new career path isn't enough. Curious conversations give you insights that you won't find on websites and articles.

I want you to commit to 50 curious conversations. You might be thinking, *that's crazy, I don't know 50 people.* But that's the point. Think of it as cross training for conversational skills. It's going to get awkward. But don't let that stop you. If you're reading this exercise right now and thinking, *oh, hell no,* it's a sign you need this exercise more than anyone.

You can complete these conversations virtually as well. The requirement is that it's a conversation, not an email or message exchange.

Start by asking people who interest you these three required questions:

- What's your job like?
- How did you get into it?
- How did you know that's what you wanted to do?

See where the conversation takes you.
There are only four rules for these conversations:

- Hide your phone.
- Look your audience in the eye.
- Ask curious questions.
- Embrace awkward.

After each conversation, reflect on the conversation. What did you learn?

After you complete the full 50 conversations, go into full reflection mode. Reflect on these questions:

- What did you learn?
- What inspired you?
- Who inspired you?
- Whose jobs would you like to have? Why?
- Whose jobs don't interest you? Why?

Assemble Your Cheer Squad

Making a career change is a vulnerable act. Any transition is full of emotion, and career transitions are no different. Sometimes you'll be stoked. Other times you'll be irritated. Sometimes you'll want to give up. During all those feels, you'll need a support system to cheer you on.

Your cheer squad is a combination of friends and professionals who will support you throughout your career transition. Find the friends who always know how to cheer you on when you're struggling. Add them to your cheer squad.

Then find your professional support system. We are living in a time with thousands of thriving professional communities, online and offline, that will welcome you as you explore and learn new skills. From organizations like Veterans in Tech to iRelaunch (a return-to-work program for mothers) to PyLadies (a group of women who love coding in Python language), these professional communities create spaces for people in career transition while also providing resources to help you learn new skills. Make professional friends with people in these types of communities and add them to your cheer squad.

The exploration process pairs best with a cheer squad. There is no reason to do a career change in isolation. Build your cheer squad as you start your career exploration.

Stay Focused with the 5-3-1 Method

Balancing the exploration process and activities with everyday life is a challenge. To stay focused and on track, use the 5-3-1 method.

The method is simple. Each week:

> Conduct **5** curious conversations
> Read **3** new job descriptions
> Pick **1** company to explore

You are free to change those numbers as you progress. You might decide on a 10-6-2 method. The point is to establish weekly goals that keep you moving forward in your exploration.

Define Your Destination Job

By this point, you've done a lot of work. Reflecting, observing, and talking. It's time to find meaning in all of that. Shaping your next career jump requires a deep dive into your learnings. From these learnings, you'll define your destination job. Destination jobs are the first job you take on your new career path.

Below are questions to help you make sense of your exploration. From the answers, you'll see a career path take shape. If you're a person who likes to talk through things, find someone to talk this out with.

Remember you're not picking a forever career. You're looking for something that you can do for the next three to five years. The answers to these questions shape your next step. To move forward, you need to identify your destination job. The destination job is the next job you'll take that sets you up on a new career path.

- What is important to you in a career?
- What industry captures your curiosity the most?
- What have you learned about the industry that captured your interest?

- What type of companies interest you?
- What job can you imagine yourself doing for the next three to five years?
- What job title fits that type of work you want to do?
- What skills are required to do that job?
- Where do you think this job will lead you in the future?
- How does this path improve your life?
- What other information do you need to make a change into a new career path?

Now, finish the sentences that kicked off this chapter.

- I want to transition into a job where I *(define type of work)*.
- I want to work for a company that *(describe type of company)*.
- I'm interested in working in an industry that *(describe the industry that interests you)*.

As your destination job takes shape, start paying attention to those who work in the industry. Read or listen to interviews about people working in your destination role or industry. Get to know their challenges. Continue reading job descriptions to understand which skills and experience you need to do your destination job. In the next section, you will learn how to get the skills you need to be qualified for your big career change.

When to Bring in the Big Guns

A book can only take you so far in the exploration phase. If you've done all the exercises, talked to all the people, and you're still just as lost, it's time to bring in the big guns. I mean a professional career coach. Because they're amazing. Having a person give you all their attention and personalized feedback about your career interests is a delight.

I didn't know the value of a career coach until I became one. I spent plenty of coaching sessions working through tough situations with clients and thinking I could have really used a career coach during tough spots in my career. If you're feeling like you can't make progress, get a coach. Get a career coach, not a life coach, unless your life is on the struggle bus too. Certifications aren't necessary. Look for coaches who have real-world coaching experience, client testimonials, and show results.

Good career coaches are cheerleaders, communicators, and connectors. A good career coach will have connections, creative ideas, and constructive feedback. They'll reflect the good and the bad in your situation and give you options for moving forward.

Ask for career coach recommendations on LinkedIn. If you're a college graduate, ask your alumni services if you can talk to someone in career services. Ask your friends if they know anyone. Many career coaches offer free consultations so you can get a sense of their coaching style and how they can (or can't) help you.

CHAPTER 7

Learning

Learning How to Learn

In my early twenties, I studied abroad in Italy. I had studied Italian in college in part because I loved the way the language sounds. On my first day in Italy, I saw an older man sitting in the town's piazza with a cute, scraggly dog. I was living my best Italian life for one single day and I wanted to talk to him. So, I strung together a sentence in Italian and worked up the confidence to speak.

I walked over to him, smiled my big American smile and told him proudly, *"Mi piece la tua carne,"* thinking that I'd just told him that I liked his dog. Unfortunately, I had mixed up the words *il cane*, for "dog," and *la carne*, for "meat." So, I told the old man I liked his meat. He looked confused and I quickly moved along. It was embarrassing. But that's how language learning works. The entire process involves throwing out a bunch of quasi-mangled words on your path to fluency. There is no other way to do it. Mistakes will be made. But that's how you learn.

I still love foreign languages. Whenever I tell someone I'm interested in learning a new language, they're quick to say that it's hard to learn a language as an adult. They follow it up by saying it's easier to learn it when you're younger. You've likely experienced this if you've ever dreamed out loud about trying to speak another language.

While it's definitely harder to learn a language as an adult, there's so much joy in learning another language at any age. It's fun to connect with someone in their language. Years after my experience in Italy, I lived in Germany for several months. I couldn't string together meaningful sentences in German, so I learned how to say the phrase "I'm the lifeguard." I wanted to say something so ridiculous and so confidently that I could get a German person's attention. It worked. Whenever I said it, I got a laugh. Often, they'd teach me something else to say, and I'd learn some more words. I made friends this way.

Learning a new language is hard. Learning how to play an instrument is hard. Learning to code is hard. Learning to speak in public is hard. Learning to write is hard. Learning to get feedback on your writing is hard.

The key thread here is that learning is hard, full stop. There's no getting around that. But learning is also playful, fun, and motivating. Even more, there is joy in learning. It feels damn good to *get it*. It's lovely to look at your progress, assess what you've learned and declare, fuck yes, I know more than what I knew two weeks ago.

Changing careers is full of learning. If you're out of the habit of learning new things, it might feel a bit odd to start learning again. You might feel stiff or dumb. That's okay. Everyone starts at the beginning when they're learning something new.

The learning party that never stops

In 2017, the *New York Times* wrote about the rise in people who are in their sunset years— 60 to 80 years old—learning to code. They profiled Ms. McKerrow, an 84-year-old who learned to code online. Helped by her grandson, she learned to code and uses her newly found tech skills to "create personalized, all-singing-and-dancing online birthday cards."[43]

What an absolute delight. I loved this story so much because it flies in the face of so much of what we tell ourselves about learning new skills. Too often we talk ourselves out of learning new things and make the excuse that we're too old to learn. It's not true, of course. You aren't too old to try to learn something new. When we say we're too old what we're really saying is, "I'm scared to try."

If you've been away from learning experiences for a while, taking on a new learning experience might seem intimidating. Traditional learning experiences have saddled us with memories of homework, bad grades, and writing papers at the last moment. These negative experiences tend to erase all the good moments. They make us forget the times when we understood a new concept so well that we could explain it to others who needed our help. The good news about learning as an adult is that grades don't matter. You can get a C in a subject, pass a course, and still get hired into a new job that pays you more than you made before.

Our culture makes trying out something new and learning a new skill as an adult seem far more high stakes than it actually is. The learning process is not high stakes. There is no requirement to be the best when you're learning. You simply need to

---

[43]*New York Times*, "Code."

show up and learn. Then you need to apply your new knowledge and your skills to something practical, so you have something to show from your learning experience.

As you customize your career and transition into an agile worker, you must integrate new learning experiences into your professional life. Lifelong learning and upskilling are the new normal. Lifelong learning is the act of consistently reflecting on your professional experience, managing your professional development, and taking advantage of opportunities to learn new skills.

Being a lifelong learner doesn't mean you need to be a student forever. Instead, it's simply seeking out opportunities, big and small, to learn new things. It's embracing your curiosity and seeking out learning experiences to enrich your professional experience.

Choose your own learning experience

As an adult, time and money are the biggest barriers to learning. Squeezing in a learning experience when work, family, and relationships demand our attention is a pain in the ass. Yet learning is the foundation of a career change. To transition into a new career, you have to elevate learning as a priority in your life.

As a career-changer, you need to pick a learning experience that fits both your lifestyle and learning style. Learning experiences are not limited to traditional classroom settings. Our generation has more access to learning opportunities and new knowledge than any prior generation. We can choose learning experiences in university classrooms, online courses, YouTube videos, mentorship, or DIY learning adventures. The opportunities to learn are endless.

Learning experiences take many different shapes, both formal and informal. Traditional career advice has driven the narrative that career changes happen through university degree programs. Bachelor's and master's degrees are paths to career transitions, but they are not the only path. They work for many people, but not all. Thankfully, you don't have to go back to school for a professional degree to make a career change. You could opt for an online certificate or create your own learning experiences if you're good at self-motivation. Your choice depends on your learning style and needs.

I struggle a lot with online learning because I like to learn with people. I prefer to be surrounded by others who are going through the process with me. Online discussion boards do not inspire me. College classrooms are amazing for that. But I also can't afford to go tens of thousands of dollars further into debt for my love of classroom discussion. I'm upskilling this time by learning Python through an online tech degree program. But I didn't just pick any online program. I searched for an online learning experience that actually offers a lively online support community and an engaging learning experience. It was hard to find, but I found the one that matches my learning style and lifestyle. The other day, I read a piece of code for the first time. I finally understood it. I felt joy.

Lifestyle learning experiences

Just like your career path should match your life needs, the learning experience you choose should match your life right now. If you can't take two years off of work to go back to school and into debt, then don't do it. If you can, make sure that learning experience will provide the outcomes you need in order to make a successful career transition.

In the next chapters, I take you through the various types of learning experiences that will help you upskill in your career change. In a career change, you aren't learning for the sake of learning. You're learning to complete a transition. To move forward in your career, you need to tie your learning experiences to your desired outcome.

You picked up this book so you could learn how to change careers. That's a good first step. But learning how to change careers isn't as simple as reading this book. You have to apply what you learn in here and practice it. Learning new skills by reading a book is like trying to learn to surf from reading a website. You can have all the knowledge, but the minute you step out there you're going to crash. It's perfectly okay to crash. But you can't quit. You have to pick your soggy-ass self up and start again. You have to take everything you learn AND throw yourself out there AND crash AND do it all over again without being the best. That's the learning process.

I'm asking you to do exactly that in this book. I want you to keep reading. But I'm about to ask you to do a lot more than just read. I'm asking you to learn by doing.

To prepare you for taking action beyond this book, I have just the exercise for you.

EXERCISE: Dance It Out

Seven years ago, I took a tango class. The reason was simple: Tango is hot and I wanted to be hot, so I signed up. I thought that after my six weeks of tango sessions I'd basically be just like Salma Hayek doing the tango in that scene from *Frida*.

I was wrong. I also had no idea what I was getting into. Learning tango meant getting intimate with strangers who were just as awkward as I was. You start chest to chest with a stranger. You're so up close and personal that the teacher gives a thorough talk on the importance of personal hygiene. The problem was that I'm really uncomfortable touching strangers. I'm not even a hugger. To find out my dream dance class involves taking cues while intimately chest to chest with a stranger was a painfully awkward experience for me. I wanted to run out of the class every time I showed up.

Unless you're a dancer, chances are dancing is awkward for you. Which is why this is the perfect exercise to kick off your learning.

I want you to take a dance class if you are able. It doesn't have to be expensive. Try one of the free ones at your community center. Drop into a bar that has free salsa lessons. Or just go to Zumba if you've never tried it before.

You might be wondering what dance has to do with career changes. It has everything to do with career changes because, in order to change, you have to take the first step: commit to learning when it feels awkward.

I want you to dance it out. You must take instruction. You must move like the instructor tells you. You must make mistakes and not dwell on mistakes. The hardest part: find joy in the process. After you complete the dance class, reflect on the following questions.

- What did you learn?
- What made you commit to this dance class?
- How did you make time for this?
- What brought you joy?

It's time to pick your dance class and get busy building your learning muscles.

Create an Experience Inventory

Understanding your work experience is a critical part of making a career transition. Before you explore which learning experiences will get you closer to your career goal, you need to understand what you already bring to the table. Your previous job titles have no reflection on your actual skill sets. No matter if you waited tables for the last four years, wrote emails all day, or entered data into a spreadsheet, you have skills. You need to get to know them. The first step to getting to know them is examining your work experience.

But first, I'd like to take this time to apologize on behalf of the entire HR industry for the bullshit résumé angst we have caused you throughout your career. Writing a résumé doesn't build your skills or help you understand your professional self. Instead, it forces you to condense your entire professional life into a cramped space, using language you'd never use in the real world. You spend hours creating a document that a recruiter will spend 10 seconds reviewing, if you get a human to review it at all.

So, ignore your résumé. Instead, create an experience inventory. An experience inventory is a list of all your jobs with a simple description of what you did in each role. The goal is to get a big-picture view of your work, free from the formal shackles of a résumé.

Your professional past is just as important as the future. With each job you take, you stack new skills on existing skills. Often, you'll find experiences in your past work that align with your future career goals.

EXERCISE: Create Your Inventory

An experience inventory is a summary of all your work in an informal list. Start by making a list of all your previous jobs. All work counts. Side hustles, volunteering, raising a family, and jobs-to-pay the bills all count as work. Use normal language. Don't include the company name. Instead, describe the type of organization you worked for. Include years, not months, to keep yourself organized. Note whether the work is contract, part-time, self-employed, or full-time.

Use a notebook or your computer but make sure you can edit. You're going to add more to this after the first round.

Below is a slice of my experience inventory as an example.

Experience Inventory

2008	(Contract Job) Long-term contract work as an administrative assistant at an insurance company
2009	Remote business development, sales, and social media marketing for an international education tech startup
2010	Program management for university global MBA programs at a business school
2012	Travel writing and digital marketing/content specialist for a luxury private jet travel company

2014   Coached and developed career work-
       shops for international MBA students,
       alumni, and executives
2017   Launched online school, designed online
       courses, taught career workshops
2018   Designed conversations for chatbots
       and analyzed conversational data

When you're done, circle the jobs you like. Strike through the ones you never want to work in again. Then reflect. What did you learn from each of these jobs?

Your experience inventory is proof of your experience and knowledge. You don't lose these things when you jump careers. You bring them with you. Examining and acknowledging them ensures you don't forget what you're capable of as you move forward. Plus, you never know when your experience from the past might help you with a new opportunity in the future.

Identify Your Skill Gap

Changing careers is like jumping into a new culture. There's a new language to learn. There are new discoveries to be made. And you feel pretty dumb as you make your way through all of it.

Feeling dumb is a normal part of a career change. Jumping into a new work world is a learning experience. Part of that experience is understanding the skills needed to succeed in the career you want. Skills are currency in the new world of work. The better you understand how your skills shape your career, the more agile you'll be.

When people ask us what we do, we share our job titles. Job titles are a tidy way of communicating all the things we do in a job. They make it easier to talk about our work. If you asked a project manager what they do and they replied, "Well, I organize projects, set deadlines, wrangle people, save money, create budgets, please stakeholders, and communicate results to management," you'd fall over in boredom. Nobody wants to hear that. So, we package it up into job titles to make everyone's life easier.

Many of us are walking around with job titles that don't make sense to anyone outside of our industry. In my last job as an MBA career coach, my title was Associate Director of Career Services. That tells you nothing about my abilities to deliver creative workshops and engage audiences of all sizes. Yet that's one of my top skills.

Relying on tidy packages to explain our work makes it harder to know what we actually do in a job. We lack the language to speak about our skills. To change careers, you must be fluent in the language of skills.

Take a skill inventory

Skills are simply the ability to do a specific task. In the context of your daily job, you use skills daily to get your job done and keep your boss happy. As a career-changer, you need to get to know your skills.

The first job you take in your new career is a destination job. To make the jump into a destination job, identify which skills you have and which skills are required for the destination job. Then note the skills you're missing. The missing skills are your skills gap. Once you know your skills gap, you'll choose a learning experience to develop the missing skills and land the destination job.

To find your skill gap, start with two lists. First, make a skill inventory. A skill inventory is simply a list of all your skills from previous jobs. Think about your previous jobs and all the tools you've used to get a job or project done. In your professional history, you've likely used a combination of technical skills and Power Skills. For example, if you work as a project manager, your skills might be: writing, managing people, building budgets, developing processes for project management software, Power-Point, and more. The goal of creating a skill inventory is to see all your skills. This is not a time to be humble. Write down every skill you use, even if you've only used it once.

Next, build a destination skills list. Destination skills are the skills needed to qualify for the destination job. Read job descriptions for your destination jobs to identify the destination skills. Job descriptions are a company's wish list of skills. Since job descriptions differ tremendously, translate them into the skills necessary to do the job.

When you have the two lists, identify which skills are missing from your skill inventory that qualify you for the destination job. The missing skills are your skill gap.

I want you to focus on identifying all your skills, no matter if you are good at them or not. For example, I'm really good at public speaking. I am not good at budgets. I have never worked with financial models. However, I have *the ability* to make a budget and I've done it several times. That's a useful skill to have if I'm transitioning into a job that requires me to work with numbers. If my destination job is a climate change analyst, I need to remember that I have worked with numbers before. It is not a brand-new skill. However, I have not created a financial model, so that would not go in my skill inventory. But, if the destination job requires that I make financial models, I would note that my lack of financial modeling is part of my skill gap. That means I'll need to make sure my learning experience includes learning financial modeling.

A career change is a strategic move. Your goal is to get a new job in a new professional path that improves your professional life. Your skill gap informs your learning experience choices. When you know which skills you are missing, you can make a plan to learn them. It ensures you select an upskilling path that teaches you the skills you need to put you on your new career path.

Once you've identified your skills gap, it's time to go shopping for your new skills.

EXERCISE: Identify Your Skills

Agile workers speak the language of skills. If you're new to looking at your work through the lens of skills, now is a good time to learn how.

Identifying your skills is like a scavenger hunt. You figure out which skills you have through a combination of reflection; conversations with coworkers; and the old standby, Google.

Start the process by revisiting your experience inventory. Review each job on your inventory list. Think about your work and tasks to get the job done. If you have a copy of old job descriptions and the résumé you submitted for the job, use them to jog your memory.

Then create a skill inventory. Reflect on the questions:

- What projects did you work on?
- What skills helped you get the work done daily?
- What software or tools did you use on a regular basis?
- What feedback from coworkers or managers have you received about your abilities?

Write down five skills that you used in each job. If you are stuck on this part, talk to former coworkers or bosses. Ask them what they think you did well. If you're still stuck, Google is there for you. There is no shortage of video explanations, skill lists, and niche websites that go into detail about the skills needed for different jobs. This final list will be your skill inventory.

Once you have a skill inventory, make a second list. On this list, write down everything that you're really good at.

Like, so good that people are always impressed. Don't be modest. Talk yourself up. This is also excellent practice for your future destination job search.

Then, circle what you love doing. When you change careers, you don't leave all your skills behind. You bring them with you. In our new world of work, employers want employees with cross-functional skills. When you know what you are able to do, you'll find more opportunities to apply your skills inside an organization. It will open up new opportunities and get you more money in the future.

Choose Your Upskill Path

Now that you speak the language of skills, it's time to figure out how to get new skills. The next section takes you through the process of evaluating different learning experiences.

There is no single path to upskilling. Traditional career advice has taught us that college degrees are the way to change careers. While college degrees offer benefits, it is not the only way to upskill. There are technical programs often offered by community colleges and apprenticeships, that teach practical skills. Careers in electrical and solar installation are lucrative career paths with a solid foundation that you don't need a college degree for. More recently, bootcamps have emerged to also serve that need. You don't need a college degree to learn to code or build a user interface for a company's app.

Remember, upskilling is the pursuit of formal and informal learning experiences to learn new skills and upgrade your career. Once you've identified where you'd like to go in your next career move, you need an upskill solution that gets you to your goal. It could be a formal college degree program. Or it could be a combination of DIY learning options and short online courses offered through your current employer. The path you choose depends on your lifestyle, financial situation, and career goals.

As you explore the options, think about how you can apply the skills and knowledge that you learn in your current job. No matter how you feel about your current place of work, they are places to apply your new knowledge and skills. When you make the jump into a new career, employers will ask for examples of how you applied your new skills. Anticipate this by finding ways to apply new skills before the job search begins. Think of it like playing with new skills. Investigate the ways you might be able to experiment within your place of work before you leave it completely.

Before you explore the upskill options, reflect on the following questions.

- What subjects interest you and what would you like to learn?
- What do you want to gain out of your learning experiences?
- How do you want to apply the new knowledge and skills that you learn?

University Degree Programs

University degree programs—both at the bachelor's and master's degree level—are a familiar path to a career change. In this section, I'm referring to traditional university degree programs completed on campus, not online (the online section comes next!). University college degrees come in all shapes and sizes. If you can afford to take on the debt or have the financial support to sustain yourself while in school, a college degree is a strong option for upskilling. The key for career-changers is to choose a program where you'll graduate with practical skills in addition to domain knowledge.

How a college degree helps career-changers

Here's the brutal truth about the American job market. There are two types of jobs: primary market jobs and secondary market jobs. Primary market jobs are the jobs that pay well; have a relatively stable schedule; and offer health benefits, the promise of upward mobility, and some career security.

Secondary market jobs are the opposite of all that. They are the temporary jobs, which are low-paying, offer no benefits, and rarely offer career progress.

A college degree is still the most common way to move from the secondary market to the primary market. Over the years, employers have engaged in a practice known as degree creep—requiring degrees for jobs that previously didn't require a college degree. While that's starting to change, not having a bachelor's degree is a barrier to the primary job market for many Americans.

By 2020, 35 percent of job openings will require at least a bachelor's degree.[44]

A bachelor's degree is useful for anyone who needs to jump from the secondary market into primary market jobs. For those looking at a master's degree as an upskill path, your career outcomes will depend on the profession.

An MBA is still the most popular master's degree. That's in part because MBAs are designed specifically for career-changers. Over 70 percent of MBA students are career-changers. Education is the second most popular, no doubt due to our need for teachers. The third most popular master's degree is in healthcare, as healthcare practitioners are required to follow a standardized curriculum to obtain their license to practice.

All three of these master's degrees map to established career paths. Outside of these subjects, however, career outcomes at the master's degree level are hit and miss. Even law degrees are suffering from an abundance of lawyers and not enough law jobs. Law graduates frequently take jobs outside of law and complain about overspending to get a law degree.

If your path to reskill is through a university degree program, choose a degree program that demonstrates the ways it improves students' professional lives after graduation.

How to make a new degree work for your career change

University degree programs have plenty to offer the curious learner. There is much joy in learning a new subject in a university setting.

---

[44]Georgetown University, "Recovery."

For career-changers, the purpose of a degree is to improve your professional situation. The biggest critique against pursuing degree programs is the number of degree programs that are not aligned with the job market needs. Pay close attention to a degree program's outcomes to make sure it's the right fit for your professional goals.

As you evaluate the programs, reflect on how you might use the degree. Ask yourself these questions:

- What will you gain from the degree?
- How will the degree program improve your access to career paths that better fit your interests?
- How much will your first job after graduation increase your current salary?
- How will this degree program improve your professional life?
- How much of your estimated monthly salary after graduation will be spent paying back your student loans?
- How will you apply the skills you are learning in class in the workplace?
- What projects will you participate in to build new skills and gain experience while in school?

If you choose the degree path, pay close attention to the job you get after you graduate. Inside Higher Ed recently reported that a study by Burning Glass Technologies found that "Bachelor's degree graduates whose first job does not require a bachelor's degree (which is how the study defines the underemployed) are significantly likelier than those whose first job did require such a degree to still be underemployed five years later."[45]

---

[45]Inside Higher Ed, "First Job."

Worse, the underemployment trend continues past five years, with some workers staying up to 10 years after college.

The job you land after college has an impact on your future career outcomes. Ask admissions representatives what career paths students take after graduation and the average starting salary. Some schools provide this data. Others do not. Choose programs that are transparent about their students' career outcomes.

As you evaluate a degree program, look for opportunities to build and apply hard skills. For example, the University of Utah recently launched a program called Degree Plus. It's an eight-week series with classes on data analysis, web design, and digital marketing. While this should be part of a college degree, not an add-on, these are the practical skills to look for in a degree program.

Lastly, choose a degree program that has a strong practical component. Make sure you have opportunities to apply your classroom learnings. Look for internship opportunities with local companies, courses where you consult with local companies on projects, and any opportunity to create something to show employers at the end of your program. Take advantage of opportunities to lead, create, and collaborate in your program to build your soft skills as you progress through the degree.

Be skeptical about for-profit colleges

For-profit colleges have a poor record when it comes to career outcomes. Recently, Corinthian Colleges was fined $30 million for lying about job placement outcomes. It later closed, but there are plenty of other for-profit colleges that sell expensive degrees wrapped in false promises of career success. For-profit degrees aren't consistently valued by employers and some institutions have made false claims about their job placement rates.

Avoid for-profit colleges that offer generic degrees in business, education, or healthcare. All of these career paths are available at community colleges for much, much cheaper. Plus, community colleges will not pressure you into enrolling. If the for-profit institution can't show you where their graduates are working or the average salary of their graduates, they are likely overstating the value of their degree.

An easy way to know if you're engaging with a for-profit college is through their sales tactics. For-profit college programs use high-pressure tactics to get you to sign up quickly. Sometimes they use emotionally exploitative sales tactics to convince you that if you don't sign up right way, you're failing yourself.

If a for-profit college degree program interests you, ask to talk to alumni about their experience finding a job, their debt, and how their degree prepared them for their new career.

An option for the truly adventurous

Pursuing a degree program outside the US is a smart option for those looking to save money and diversify their experience. Over the past decade, countries have built English degree programs to internationalize their universities. There are plenty of degree programs open to Americans who want to live and learn abroad.

I completed my master's degree in Denmark on a Danish government scholarship. My tuition was free and I received a monthly stipend. Several countries offer free tuition—Germany is one of them. Many others like France, Sweden, and Scotland offer English language degree programs that are cheaper than what you'll find in the US. Most employers will not care where you received a degree (unless you're pursuing law or medicine, then there are rules).

Choosing this option is the ultimate adventure. You'll learn alongside people from different parts of the world and experience different educational models. More importantly, you'll experience so many new possibilities that you won't get by staying in the US. And, if you want to work in another country after graduation, a degree in your target country is the way to go.

Online Learning

Online degrees and courses are expanding rapidly as an alternative to traditional, campus-based university degree programs. The obvious advantage of online learning experiences is flexibility: you get the freedom to learn from anywhere. As a career-changer, you have access to stand-alone courses, degree programs, and learning communities at a fraction of the cost of a traditional university education. You don't even have to put on pants to learn all the things.

With so much choice, it's easy to fall into analysis paralysis. So, let's break this down. The online learning paths that matter most for career-changers: online degrees, skill-based programs, and stand-alone courses.

Online degrees

Universities have expanded and improved their online degrees in the past decade. Additionally, online learning platforms like

Coursera and edX also offer online degrees in collaboration with universities like Harvard, MIT, Columbia, and more. If you want a university degree but can't take the time off work, online degrees are ideal. In most cases, an online degree is more affordable than a campus-based degree.

Coursera partners with universities to offer affordable degree options. For example, an online MBA from the University of Illinois offered through Coursera is about $22,000. The same MBA program on campus costs $57,618. While the online option through Coursera isn't cheap, you're still eligible for financial aid through the online option.

Western Governors University is an innovative online learning model in a category of its own. This organization gets a special mention here, as it's a fully accredited, nonprofit university that operates entirely online (read: not a shady for-profit institution that'll leave you in debt with a worthless online degree). You'll get quality instruction designed for online learners because their university is built for online learners. The average cost of a bachelor's degree from Western Governors University is $15,000. According to their website, the average student loan debt of WGU graduates in 2017 was less than half the national average.

Skill-based programs

An alternative to a fully online degree program is a short-term, online skill-building program. These are online programs that build digital skills to help you level up in your career. They take less time to complete than a fully online degree and place a focus on learning the digital skills that give you greater flexibility in your career.

The terminology for these programs varies depending on the company. The online learning platform, Treehouse Learning, calls them Tech degrees, while Skillcrush calls them Career Blueprints. Udacity calls them Nano Degrees. While these programs are not degrees in the traditional sense—they're not offered by an accredited institution—they offer packages of courses that are ideal for career-changers.

Skillcrush is an online school that offers three-month digital skills training courses with a money-back guarantee. You can upskill into in-demand careers like visual design, user experience (UX), and front-end development. Each student completes a project and a portfolio, so they have tangible proof of their new skills.

Udacity's Nano Degrees are similar in that students build projects and portfolios. Udacity's programs are measured into weeks, so you get a sense of how much time per week you'll spend in class. For their Predictive Analytics for Business class, you'll study 10 hours a week for three months.

edX takes a slightly different approach to helping the masses upskill. edX offers MicroMasters, which are skill-based degrees offering "pathways to today's top jobs." The degrees are offered through a partnership with a host university but built through employer collaboration. Each degree program is "validated" by top companies. Career-changers can choose from a range of MicroMasters from design thinking to artificial intelligence to digital marketing.

As an added bonus, participants in edX MicroMasters programs may choose to continue their studies on campus at the host institution. For example, if you complete a MicroMasters in Digital Product Management offered in partnership with Boston University, you're eligible to apply to Boston University

Questrom School of Business, putting you on a path to earn a Master of Science degree in Digital Innovation. The credits you earn in the MicroMasters are already credited toward your on-campus degree. MicroMasters degrees are like a test run for the full master's degree.

All of the skill-based programs above offer learning and career support alongside their course instruction.

Stand-alone courses

Stand-alone courses are online courses that help you learn a specific skill. There are hundreds of thousands of online courses to choose from. Sites like Udemy and Skillshare are full of courses to help you learn new skills. You'll find everything from Ink Drawing to Creative Writing to Excel Skills. LinkedIn Learning is another big player in this space. With classes like Advertising on Instagram to Creating Video for a Non-Profit, LinkedIn Learning offers "courses for every step of your career." If you want to learn it, chances are it's on one of these sites.

A standout example is freeCodeCamp. This nonprofit provides online coding courses for free. They offer a worldwide community of learners, open source projects to help you apply your coding skills, and hundreds of YouTube tutorials to support you.

While useful for learning one-off skills, stand-alone courses aren't ideal for career-changers who need a structured learning path. Stand-alone courses aren't part of a program or developed in concert with employer needs. They also might not have a portfolio component or career support. If you are the type of person who's a self-directed learner and good at creating your own learning path, these courses might be an ideal learning experience for you.

Choosing the right online learning experience for career-changers

Choosing an online program takes some investigative work. There are five categories to consider when searching for an online program that supports your career transition:

- Length of program
- Cost
- Learning style
- Practical project experience
- Career support

The length of program should match the timing of your career transition. When do you want to start your new career?

Next, what can you afford? Most online programs cost money. Some obviously more than others. Luckily, some offer financial aid. Tech-based skill programs in particular are eager to get more women and minorities into tech fields in which they're underrepresented, so some of them offer scholarships.

Then think about your learning style. Do you want a supportive, engaged learning community? Are you good plowing through the material on your own or need a 1:1 interaction with the instructor? How do you prefer to discuss materials—through forums, Slack channels, or video chat? The answers to these questions will help you find a learning experience that matches your style.

Always look for practical projects when choosing an online learning path. Ideally, the online program you choose will provide an opportunity to work on an employer-sponsored project. The value of online learning is that the programs tend to be career-focused and provide project-based learning. If you're just passively reading materials and not applying them, you're not going to build the skills you need to show future employers. You can't learn to code by reading a website!

Lastly, look for programs with career support. This book is a fabulous resource. But I can't be there to coach you through everything. Find a program that gives you career guidance, whether it's résumé help, mentorship, interview preparation, or connections to local employers.

For example, Skillcrush offers a Break into Tech program ideal for career-changers who don't have a tech background. In the 12-month program you'll take interactive classes to learn digital skills and make a "built-from-scratch personal portfolio website to use on the job search" and produce "three professional-quality web projects to show off."[46] On top of that, you get access to their alumni community and meetings with a career counselor. It's a good option for $1,599, which is about $130 a month.

Finding the right online learning experience in the sea of online learning options takes time and research. Take your time and go deep to learn if online learning experiences will be your ideal learning path.

Community College

Community colleges are an overlooked path for career-changers, especially among graduates from four-year universities. Community colleges are often considered the more affordable path to a college degree. They provide general education requirements in a flexible, accessible environment. I started my college

---

[46]Skillcrush, "Break Into Tech Blueprint."

experience at a community college. It wasn't fancy. But it was flexible. I worked full-time during the day and went to school at night, later transferring to a four-year school.

Community colleges are more than a path to a four-year degree. Increasingly, community college is an ideal learning path for career-changers. Students are graduating from two-year community college programs with job-ready skills in cutting-edge industries. Many community colleges offer short-term programs that map to high paid jobs, no four-year degree necessary.

For example, Portland Community College offers a certificate in Cybersecurity. All courses in the program map to "knowledge units of the National Security Agency and the Department of Homeland Security requirements for a Center of Academic Excellence in Cyber Defense 2-Year Education."[47] Translation: you'll exit this program ready to work at a government-level job in cybersecurity. According to the Herjavec Group, a leading global security consulting firm, there will be 3.5 million unfilled cybersecurity positions by 2021. But it doesn't take a global advisory firm to tell you that, with massive data breaches happening monthly, companies desperately need cybersecurity professionals. The median salary for a cybersecurity specialist in 2016 was $92,600, but went as high as $140,000 a year.

If cybersecurity isn't your thing, that's cool. Community colleges are partnering with local employers to develop technical programs that meet employer needs. Lorraine Community College in Ohio offers a Micro Electromechanical Systems (MEMS) Short-Term Certificate. Students learn in the cleanroom and get hands-on experience working with "materials, equipment, protocols, and processes related to the microelectronics industry."

---

[47]Portland Community College, "Computer Information Systems."

Students exit the program with some serious skills: "sensor and microcircuit operation, material and size constraints, microelectronic packaging, printed circuit design, manufacturing, and project management."[48] The same community college also offers short-term certificates and associate degrees in automation engineering—preparing workers to work on autonomous systems for autonomous cars, 3D electronics design, and alternative energy.

The list of cutting-edge training programs at community colleges goes on. There are programs for drone technology operators, robotics, project management, entrepreneurship, and more.

Another advantage of community college programs is that they accept anyone. Seriously. No admissions bullshit here. You want to learn? Great, you're in. Plus, taking a community college course creates a habit of learning. If you've been out of the learning experience for a while, attending a class at your community college will help you ease back into things.

With flexible courses during the evening and on weekends, community colleges are truly an ideal environment to learn to reskill. Plus, you'll learn from people with different economic, social, political, and racial backgrounds. You'll get outside of your bubble and really, we all need a lot more of that right now.

Community colleges are places to start exploring your career change options if you're not sure what your next step is. Unlike traditional university certificate programs, community college certificate programs are tied to local employment demand. Community colleges, as their name suggests, are pillars of their community. They partner with local employers to train up an in-demand workforce. They play a significant role in efforts to help people reskill and transition into new career paths.

---

[48]Lorain County Community College, "Micro Electromechanical Systems."

Check in with your local community college to learn what programs they offer. You might be surprised.

Bootcamps

Bootcamps are fast-paced programs that teach digital skills to people without a technical skills foundation. The beauty of bootcamps is that they're designed specifically for people who want to upskill. With the goal of helping working professionals acquire digital skills, they are ideal for anyone who wants a skill and salary upgrade. While they're a newer, alternative learning experience compared to traditional degree programs, they've evolved as one of the quickest ways for working professional to acquire foundational digital skills.

Bootcamps originally started as places to learn to code. Their existence filled an immediate need for employers who needed workers with digital skills. Prospective students could choose from learning experiences like front-end web development or back-end development. Front-end developers make the stuff you see online look good and work seamlessly. Back-end developers work on the technology behind the scenes that you don't see: databases, servers, and the application itself. Students can also learn how to become a mobile app developer, as many bootcamps offer iOS and Android app development paths.

All of these skills are highly in demand in the workplace. Front-end developers average around $75,000 a year. More importantly though, they have the foundational knowledge and skills to progress in a digital workplace.

Bootcamp learning experiences are no longer limited to coding skills. They've since evolved to teach the skills that prepare workers for tech-adjacent roles in user experience (UX) design, user interaction (UI) design, data analytics, digital marketing, and data science.

Understanding financial aid for bootcamps

Bootcamps aren't accredited like universities and colleges, so most will not be eligible for federal financial aid. Some bootcamps offer loans through partnerships with loan providers. Others are experimenting with income-based repayment options, commonly known as an ISA (Income Share Agreement). This financial model means students pay nothing through their education program and only pay after they start a job. The percentage you pay is set before you start the program. You may also pay more on a repayment based on your subject of study.

Lambda School is an all-online coding school that teaches computer science, iOS app development, and data science to career-changers. They offer an income-based repayment option instead of taking out a loan or paying $20,000 for their education. Currently, students pay no money at the start of the program and pay 17 percent of their salary for two years, with a $30K maximum total payment.

The ISA is emerging as a popular financial aid model for bootcamps and short-term skill programs. Much like taking out student loans has pros and cons, so does an ISA. In many cases, the ISA debt is held by Wall Street, which pools and trades the debt. While an ISA may allow you to upskill into a new career without paying up front, the jury is out on how Wall Street will treat you long-term if you fall behind on repayment. So, take time to research your expected salary at graduation, pay attention to the interest rate, and always read the fine print of any ISA.

As bootcamps are still relatively new to the continuing education scene, it's important to take time to research boot-camp options. They are for-profit education systems with little government oversight. There is still debate on how well coding bootcamps prepare workers for high-paying jobs. As new boot-camps enter the market daily, and others close down due to lack of revenue, the quality of bootcamps varies greatly. SwitchUp and Course Report are excellent tools to see the rankings and feedback on bootcamps.

Choosing the right bootcamp

Similar to online programs, these are the things that you need to look for when choosing a bootcamp:

- Free intro course
- Program details and syllabus
- Cost
- Learning style
- Practical project
- Career support
- Alumni outcomes

Many bootcamps offer a free intro course to understand their teaching style and find out if learning these digital skills is a right fit for you. For example, Lambda School offers a free online course for beginners with no coding experience. Participants learn the basics of code and an introduction to the programming language JavaScript.

Unlike traditional degree programs, bootcamps should show you exactly what you'll learn in their programs. General Assembly is a global leader among bootcamps. For every program on their website, you'll learn about career support, financial aid options, price, syllabus, instructors, and projects that you'll work on. This level of transparency is important; these are fast-paced, short-term programs. You need to know what skills you'll learn, who you'll learn from, and what work you'll be able to do after graduation. You need to know exactly what you're getting before you buy.

Examining bootcamp learning styles

Bootcamps are intensive programs. You will learn a lot of information and new skills in a short amount of time. Much like online degree programs, there is a variety of learning experiences and instructors between schools. In some schools, you work on your own. Others pair you with a mentor. Other bootcamps pair you with a partner to learn together, increasing the chances you can troubleshoot technical issues together. Take time to learn about the pace of the program, the learning community, and homework expectations outside of class.

Most instructors are industry professionals. But just because they're professionals doesn't mean they can teach! Spend time learning about the instructor's background and don't skip the free intro course.

Bootcamps are designed for building skills, so every boot-camp program should result in a project, ideally one that is built with employer or industry collaboration. Lambda School includes four weeks of Lambda Labs, where students partici-pate in an "In-House Apprenticeship by building a real-world project in a small team."[49] Participants in General Assembly's Software Engineering Immersive program graduate with a portfolio of completed projects developed in collaboration with employers.

Bootcamps offer on-campus and online options. Take time to figure out which one fits your schedule and learning style best. Check the length of programs that match your career transition goals. Some bootcamps offer part-time programs in the evening, while others are full-time, 9 to 5 classes.

As bootcamps are designed for career-changers, they should offer career support. Some might offer job placement. Oth-ers might have connections and offer a hiring pipeline to local employers. A good bootcamp offers access to mentors and indus-try professionals and teaches you how to build contacts in your new field.

Inquire about career support and job placement during the admissions process. Ask to talk to alumni about their job search experience. Since the quality between bootcamps varies, ask bootcamp graduates how employers reacted to their quali-fications and new skills. Ask them how they made their career transition too.

If the bootcamps can't offer you anyone who can speak to the learning and job search experience, the bootcamp isn't a good fit for you.

---

[49]Lambda School, "User Experience Design."

Certificate Programs

Upskilling through certificate programs is a growing path for many career-changers. Certificate programs have exploded in popularity over the years, especially as universities seek to offer shorter, more affordable programs to working professionals. While affordability varies by institution and program, certificates are cheaper than a full degree program. Plus, you can qualify for financial aid to pay for certificates offered through accredited universities.

The data on career outcomes from non-degree credentialing— i.e., certificate holders—is hard to come by. Employers' attitudes toward certificate holders are difficult to pin down, which makes it hard to know if certificates hold their value in the market.

Certificate programs are useful for career-changers who need to understand the vocabulary and systems in a new industry. They provide a short, direct path to learn as much as possible about a new industry. But when it comes to skill development and career outcomes, certificate programs are hit and miss.

Recently, I came across a certificate in Higher Education Administration from Northwestern. For $19,975, I can "deepen (my) understanding of the field and expand (my) networks."[50] Details on career outcomes or paths are notably absent. Instead, the page offers the basics of college career services: "ongoing professional development support, one-on-one career coaching, academic advising, and networking opportunities." There was nothing to reassure me that investing $20,000 into a certificate program will make me more employable. The lack of testimonials

---

[50]Northwestern, "SESP."

from employers raving about the certificate or explaining how the certificate signaled a candidate's competitiveness on the open job market, was telling.

Certificates are not certifications

Certificates are not the same as certifications, though you'd be forgiven for mixing them up. It's easy to think a university certificate in higher education administration will provide the same salary bump as a Cisco Certified Network Professional certification (it doesn't). The former is a revenue generation program from a university with little focus on skill building and an unclear career trajectory. The latter is an industry-approved career training model with clearly defined career paths.

In a 2018 report by Burning Glass Technologies titled "The Narrow Ladder: The Value of Industry Certifications in the Job Market," they defined certifications as "awarded by a certifying body, often an industry association or trade group, based on an examination process assessing whether an individual has acquired the designated knowledge, skills, and abilities to perform a specific job."[51] This differs from certificates, which the report defines as "short-term, professionally oriented credentials awarded by an educational institution (as opposed to an industry body) based on completion of specific coursework." The same report found that in 2015, around 1.5 million job postings required certifications, whereas only about 130,000 postings required certificates.

---

[51] Burning Glass Technologies, "The Narrow Ladder."

Translation: certifications are proof of your ability to do a job whereas certificates are proof of domain knowledge. Certificates and certifications are used interchangeably but they are not the same. Certifications are more valued by employers in the marketplace than certificates. As a career-changer, certificates may not hold the value you expect them to hold in the job search.

How to make a certificate work for your career change

Certificate programs are revenue-generating programs for universities, so you have to get beyond the marketing hype and do a bit of digging to find out if a certificate helps you develop the skills for a career change. Use these questions to guide you:

- Does the certificate add to or improve your power skills?
- Does the certificate improve your technical skills?
- Does the certificate position you for a hybrid job?
- Has the certificate been developed with industry or employer input?
- Does this certificate frequently appear as a requirement in job postings?
- Will you learn skills in this program that will still be relevant in five years?
- Does the institution offering the certificate offer connections to employers?

Certificates do not convey the same value as a college degree to employers, even if a certificate is offered by a brand name school. If you are considering a certificate program, ask smart questions and conduct deep research to learn exactly how a certificate prepares you for your career jump.

Make sure the certificate program you choose helps you build the skills you need for your destination job and makes you a competitive candidate in the job search.

Workplace Learning

One of the most overlooked ways to build new skills is your own workplace. I'm all for a fresh start, but sometimes there are magical opportunities in your own professional backyard. And sometimes they're free.

Get to know learning experiences offered at your workplace. Start by checking out what's happening in your HR department. You probably haven't thought about them since you signed all those forms at the start of your job, but they're home to a lot of resources. Check out the internal employee website and look for training options like mentorship programs, upcoming workshops, and internal trainings. Some employers offer free subscriptions to online learning platforms, like LinkedIn Learning. While we've left the glory baby boomer days where employers covered employee tuition, there are a handful of companies that offer tuition reimbursement. For example, Starbucks currently offers free tuition for Arizona State University's online degree program.

Next, ask your boss what professional development options you're eligible for. Better yet, come prepared. Find a conference in your industry. Professional conferences are filled with workshops and talks that introduce you to trends in your field. Ask your boss if there's money in the budget to send you to a conference. If you're more advanced in your career, ask your boss if they'd cover an executive program like an Exec MBA or a tech-focused degree.

Asking for the opportunity to learn shows your boss you're interested in your professional development. Employers love that. Make these asks for professional development even if you're planning to leave your job. Do not feel guilty. I know that's taboo but remember, employers are replaceable. Take advantage of every training opportunity they provide. You never know, you might learn so much in your company that you end up getting a job offer and a raise. So, get busy asking.

Lastly, get yourself on a project where you have to learn and use a new set of skills. Bonus points if it's on a project outside of your own department. Find a project where you're building or producing something of value like a piece of software, a new marketing campaign, a workshop, or a new data set. Challenge yourself to take on a role that's normally outside of your comfort zone. Hate speaking in public? Build your skills by offering to present the results of your project to management. Project work teaches you how to apply new skills and builds collaboration skills. You might discover you're really good at something that you'd never done before.

Your workplace may be full of learning opportunities. Take advantage of them and experiment in your workplace.

DIY Learning

I'm obsessed with a series on YouTube called CrashCourse. CrashCourse dives deep into a range of subjects like physics, philosophy, economics, biology, literature, data science, and more. With nearly a billion views, I'm not the only one who finds this content useful. The Pew Research firm found that 37 percent of all millennials tap into career development content on YouTube. YouTube is obviously a go-to place for learning, but so are podcasts, free online courses, and email newsletters. We're in the glory days of DIY learning. The trick is learning how to use all this content to fuel your DIY learning path.

To build your own DIY learning adventure, start with your desired professional outcome and work backward. What domain knowledge and skills do you want to learn? Then investigate your resources. As you discover opportunities to learn something new, look for credibility. What background does this person have to be an authority on the subject? Are they trying to sell you something? Are they making promises that are too good to be true? Do they have testimonials?

Next, find a way to apply the skills you're learning. Reading and watching videos is passive learning. While you'll get valuable information, you still need to apply what you're learning to build new skills. Either find a project at work or create a project of your own. For example, Harvard put their famous computer science course on YouTube. The nine-lecture series gives an overview of algorithms and data structures, as well as an introduction to coding languages like Python, JavaScript, and CSS. While you won't learn to code from this class, it's a great start to understanding coding and the technology that underpins our daily lives. Plus, it'll help you figure out what programming language you might want to learn.

Combining the Harvard YouTube series with a free resource like Codeacademy, a free online school that teaches people how to code, is an affordable way to learn to upskill.

At the very least, start writing about what you're learning. The process of summarizing your learning builds skills. You'll learn how to write concisely. You'll build knowledge management skills that you can use in future jobs. Seeking out information and making sense of it is an in-demand skill.

In the job search, you're going to have to show how apply your new knowledge and skills. Simply telling an employer, "I read some articles and watched a few YouTube videos, hire me," doesn't cut it. Showing them what you've learned, either through your writing or self-driven projects, will make you stand out. Practice communicating your new learnings and you will be well on your way to nailing your destination job interview.

Making a career change with DIY learning

Start by making a personal learning syllabus for yourself. A personal learning syllabus keeps you organized and focused. Map out a timeline for learning a new skill. Set a learning goal for each week that gets you closer to that goal. Include what you'll learn each week and list the resource that you'll learn from.

Next, build your habit. Choosing the DIY learning approach requires more self-discipline than other learning experiences. It's easy to flake on yourself. It's also easy to end up down a YouTube rabbit hole that has nothing to do with what you're learning. Commit to distraction-free learning for 30 minutes to one hour each day. Commit to giving yourself space to dive into the learning experience, free from other distractions.

Finally, find a community of people to support your learning. Whether it's a Facebook or Slack group, a meet up, or just friends who are also into learning, find your people. Learning together is more motivational than learning alone. Share your learning goals and struggles.

Many career-changers include DIY learning alongside other learning experiences. For example, if you've heard that data science is the top-paying career in the US but don't know anything about data science, it's worth watching a few videos about data science before signing up at a data science bootcamp.

Make DIY learning a professional habit

The future belongs to those who continue to learn throughout their career. Use tactics from DIY learning to keep exploring trends and ideas in your industry, even after your career change. It's easy to do. Imagine replacing 15 minutes of social media scrolling with 15 minutes of listening to an industry podcast or watching a quick tutorial on a skill related to your job. Imagine what you'd learn after a month or year. Upskilling habits like these create agile workers, introduce you to future opportunities, and keep your skills relevant in a fast-changing world of work.

EXERCISE: Choose Your Own Learning Path

Now that you've explored the variety of learning experiences, it's time to make a choice.

Answer the following questions:

- What skills do you want to learn?
- What is your preferred learning style?
- What learning experience(s) can you afford?
- Which learning path best fits your lifestyle right now?
- Which learning path gets you the most excited to learn?
- Which learning path best supports your career transition goals?
- Which learning path gives you the skills you need for your destination job?

Use your answers to narrow down the options. If you have more than one option, organize the options. Make a list of learning experiences that interest you.

- How long are the programs that interest you?
- How much do they cost?
- Can you talk to someone to learn more?

Finally, make the choice based on what you can afford, your timelines, and career goals.

Create Space to Upskill

Now comes the hard part. Once you've selected and committed to your learning path, it's time to make time to learn. Finding time to learn is a challenge for most working adults. It's not easy. But you can do it. You're going to be fighting the twin monsters every day: procrastination and distraction.

The good news is that you can win the battles. Start by establishing a daily learning commitment to yourself. Make a list of what you need to accomplish for your learning task that day. Learning how to learn is part of the learning process. Depending on your lifestyle, this may be the hardest part about learning. It takes about a month to develop the habit of learning. Don't give up.

Next, find an environment that works best for you to learn. Keep away from distractions like TV and people. In 2018, the average US adult spent four hours and 46 minutes per day watching TV, according to the Nielsen Total Audience Report.[52] If you can, avoid working from home where distractions like family, TV, and chores creep into your learning experience time. Maybe you go to a cafe. Maybe it's the library. Or maybe you just need to lock yourself in a well-lit closet. Wherever it is, find it and claim it.

Now, slay the distraction monster. Silence your phone. Turn off all the dings and vibrations. Each time you get a ding, you interrupt your focus. Silence it all. Then sign out of all social media. These apps were designed to keep us scrolling and checking for notifications. Don't assume you're stronger than the pull of social media. Hide your phone while you work.

---

[52]Nielsen, "Time Flies."

Once you're set up, focus on the process. Even if you can only do 15 minutes at a time, commit to the 15 minutes. If you've got an hour, make the most of it. Each time you carve space for your learning experience, pay attention to what makes you focus, when you get into your groove, and where you get stuck.

Throughout the learning process, people will still want your time. Kids in particular force people to become time management wizards, cramming in learning wherever they can. You might need to find additional solutions to balancing learning and childcare. It isn't easy for everyone. Ask for help where possible. Since household chores, childcare, and eldercare duties fall heavily on women's shoulders, women often have less time to engage in learning pursuits. If you're in this situation, tell your partner to step up their game. If they don't, remind them that you're learning how to change and once you've got that badass new career you might just change them up too.

CHAPTER 8

Searching

Don't Fear the Job Search

Congratulations, you have emerged from your career transition and are ready to tackle the job search. The first job search in a career jump is tough. But I'm here to tell you that you're going to get through this and shine on the other side.

Job searches suck. You can expect rejection, or worse, silence for all your hard efforts. You're walking right into it. But that's okay. You can handle this. Because you're bold as fuck.

Bold is your vibe as you march into the job search process and claim your space. Bold is the person who's able to take risks and have courage. You're bold because you've already done a ton of work. You've built conversational skills and taught yourself how to learn new skills. Be proud. You are more than ready for the job search. You've earned it.

You're not starting over. You're bringing perspective, experience, new ways of thinking, and fresh skills to any new job you want.

Rejection is not failure

The job search is a negative experience for many people. ERE Media, an industry resource for human resources and recruiting professionals, reported on a study by Indeed. In a survey of 10,000 job seekers worldwide, the researchers found that "Two-thirds (65 percent) of respondents worry others will find out they are looking for a new job."[53] The study also found that "two thirds (64 percent) said they feel anxious when searching for a new job, half feel secretive, and a third even feel like they're leading a double life." Also, 52 percent wouldn't tell a partner when applying for a role and 52 percent also said their biggest concern was work colleagues finding out about their job search.

The collective angst about job searching is partially rooted in our fear of failure. The job search is an act of vulnerability. Summoning up your confidence and throwing yourself at an employer in hopes they choose you is a vulnerable act. We don't think about it that way because we all have to get jobs, so we have to go through the dreadful search on autopilot. Each time you submit your professional documents, the ones that you've worked hard to craft but don't actually represent your true self, you open yourself up to rejection. This vulnerability fuels our fear of failure.

We mix up rejection with failure, but rejection is not failure. Failure is staying in a job that you don't like and not moving forward. But you've already succeeded in moving forward and learning new skills. You're at the last stage of your career jump. Even if you get rejected by 50 companies at this stage, you haven't failed (though you may want to try something different).

---

[53]ERE, "Social Media."

Rejection in the job search is simply an employer telling you that you aren't a match. It sucks, but it is not failure.

Your vulnerability is only one half of the story. Employers are mighty callous when it comes to your vulnerability. They've built a brutal selection process, one that screams *we don't give a fuck about your feelings*. It's only going to get worse as companies move toward a hiring process that's more automated and less human.

Get your battle gear on

You will get rejected in your job search. Plan for it because the reality is that there are too many applications for every opening. Rejection isn't always a reflection on your ability to do a job; sometimes it's just a numbers game. A recruiter I follow on LinkedIn shared a post about why it takes her so long to respond to candidates. She summarized what happens behind the scenes after you submit:

- 150 people applied on Indeed
- 100 people applied through LinkedIn
- 50 applied on the company website
- 2 people applied internally
- 2 people were referred by employees
- The recruiter has 60 other people who she's reached out to and must respond to

Every recruiter is trying to sort through the pile of résumés to find the golden candidate. With résumé loads like that, recruiters are spending less than 10 seconds looking at your résumé.

Once I listened to a recruiter tell a group of new students that he only phone screens the first 20 applications that come in. On average, they get over 200 applications per position. Honestly, it's a miracle any of us get hired with these odds and practices.

My friends, the hiring odds are not in your favor. There are so many things you can't control in the job search. I've over-heard colleagues reject qualified candidates for stupid things like lack of an Ivy League degree or leaving a job after a year and a half. Once, an employer I was interviewing with asked my for-mer boss during the reference check how loud I was in the office. (Full disclosure: I am a loud person.) I ended up getting the job, but I always wondered what would have happened if my former boss had said I was too loud. Would I have got the job? The peo-ple hiring you are picky as fuck.

They are biased too. When I was 19, I worked in the back of a print shop. The owner refused to let women learn how to use the four-color printing machines. Instead, we could only learn how to collate and bind books. When I was a staffing recruiter, some clients would insist on hiring only women for their front desk positions. While we reminded them that it was illegal to do so and sent them candidates from both, they only hired women. My experiences are a small drop in the bucket of bias that individuals experience in the hiring process.

People of color, women, older people, LGBTQ, and non-gender-conforming individuals experience loads of discrimi-nation in the hiring process. In 2017, the Proceedings for the National Academy of Sciences in the United States of America conducted a study to "assess trends in hiring discrimination against African Americans and Latinos over time."[54] The result

---

[54]PNAS, "Discrimination."

of the study found that "Since 1989, whites receive on average 36 percent more callbacks than African Americans, and 24 percent more callbacks than Latinos." Age discrimination is an enduring problem in the job search too, with the AARP reporting that "44 percent of older job applicants say they have been asked (illegally) for age-related information from potential employers."[55]

Discrimination in the job search is real and it's not fair. I tell you this not to dissuade you but to encourage you to keep fighting. The job search is a cold-ass process that doesn't give a fuck about meritocracy or even your feelings. So, it's perfectly acceptable to hate the job search process. But don't let the fear of rejection prevent you from going after your destination job as if it's already yours.

Get your battle gear on. Focus on what you can control in the hiring process. Make sure that every time you engage with a potential employer you present as the strongest candidate possible. Don't settle for shitty employers. The way an employer treats you in the hiring process is often reflective of how they'll treat you as an employee. So, find companies that treat you well in the recruiting process; they're out there. I'm cheering for you from afar because I want you to get hired so you can change the way we treat job seekers from the inside out.

In light of all the messiness in hiring, it's time to reframe rejection as a badge of experience. Use rejection as a chance to learn. If an employer gives you silence, try something different next time. If you find yourself saying "I've submitted 50 résumés and nothing is happening!" it's time to reflect and try something different—like creating a website, reevaluating your qualifications for the job, or making a human connection.

---

[55]AARP, "Age Discrimination."

You are not your job. Your worth is not tied to whether or not employers respond to your résumé or interview skills. Sometimes it's just a matter of timing. Other times it's a matter of communicating your skills right. The job search is a game of persuasion. If you're not skilled in persuasion, then you'll need to build that skill as you look for a job.

Be kind to yourself in this process. Rejection sucks. Acknowledge it and learn from it. Find a friend to rant to about it and keep moving forward.

Translate Your Skills

The job search is an act of persuasion. Your goal is to persuade an employer that you are the best person for the job. In an ideal world, the best person for a job would be the person who has the most skills to do the job. But we don't live in an ideal world. In reality, the person who communicates their abilities the best gets the job. Notice the distinction. The job search is about communicating your skills and experience, not just having the right skills.

As you approach the job search, remember to speak the language of skills. You must communicate what you are able to do for a company. Your abilities are everything that you have learned during your learning experience, plus any relevant skills that you had prior to your career change. Don't forget to communicate any relevant skills from previous work experiences as qualifications for the destination job. Stack your skills.

Before your job search, revisit your skill inventory. Update it with all the skills you gained in your learning experience. Note any projects that you completed during your learning experience that show an employer you have new skills.

Translating your skills into a language employers understand is a creative act. It requires that you get beyond only submitting résumés. Experiment by telling stories that show off your new skills, creating digital portfolios that show off your projects, and personal websites that communicate your work and abilities. You're at the top of your game right now, fresh off a learning experience. Go after it.

Make a Human Connection

The job search has a habit of getting people down. It's common to hear people share job search stories that go like this: "I've submitted over 50 résumés and I haven't heard anything." That's a lot of résumés, but what always gets me is the last part: *I haven't heard anything.*

That's loneliness talking. Sending your professional documents off into the void and getting no response is a lonely process. Doing it over and over again, 20, 50, 100 times, only makes the process lonelier. The lonelier we get, the more we retreat from talking about our job search and connecting with others. The result is discouragement and loss of motivation.

You must interrupt the loneliness. You need human connection in the job search. As more companies try to automate people out of the hiring process—by use of interview chatbots and recorded interviews with no human present—human connection is even more important in your job search. Talking to people about their experiences, asking a recruiter about a job opening, or sharing your struggles with your community are all opportunities to make a human connection. Sometimes they benefit you too.

In the exploration section I challenged you to talk to 50 people about their professional experience. The primary goal of those conversations was to help you discover future careers and insights that you wouldn't get from reading a website. There was an alternative goal too: to build your conversational skills for the job search.

When I talk to job seekers, I always ask them "Who are you talking to in your job search?" Most job seekers are baffled by the question. Nobody, is a common answer. It shouldn't be.

There are three types of people to talk with throughout your job search: your power squad, recruiters, and your cheerleaders.

Your power squad is a group of people who are working in jobs or careers that interest you. These are often strangers who you haven't met. These people work inside of companies in industries or roles that interest you. Build your power squad by reaching out to these people. Using LinkedIn or an email, introduce yourself and ask to have a short conversation about their work. During the conversation, listen to their experiences and ask curious questions. You'll get insights and feel motivated by the conversation. They might even keep you in mind for future job openings.

Recruiters are the gatekeepers to the companies where you want to work. When you see a job that interests you, send them an email with a smart question or two about the job you want. Ask them about the position and put your LinkedIn profile link in the email so they can look you up. Let them know you're interested.

Cheerleaders are your support crew. Every job seeker needs a support crew. Cheerleaders will tell you how good you are but will also keep you in check if you aren't putting your best self forward. Everyone has cheerleaders. Find yours. Talk to them when it gets hard.

It's easy to avoid human interaction in the job search. Fight the urge to do so and start talking to people. You'll feel more motivated and you never know where the conversation might lead.

How to Leave A Job

I've worked in a lot of crappy jobs. More than once, I've fantasized about flipping a table, telling everyone to fuck off, and exiting in a blaze of glory. Anyone who's ever been in a job they hate has had a similar fantasy. Unfortunately, these days an act like that will land you on BuzzFeed, wrecking your Google search results forever.

Most people choose the quiet path: simply keep quiet and exit without making waves. Give your two weeks, share your contact details with the coworkers you like, and peace out without going viral.

There is, however, a third, more strategic way to leave your job. It's a way that sets you up for a future of career jumps. It's called the vampire exit. Before you give your notice, suck your employer dry of all relationships and knowledge that's useful to you. It sounds more morbid than it really is. But stay with me here.

Before you announce that you're quitting, start building relationships with interesting people at your work. Set up casual but covert coffee meetings for chats. Take advantage of any free training opportunities. Seek out small opportunities to learn and apply a new skill before you leave. When you've drained the organization of interesting people and training opportunities, then announce your official exit.

The vampire exit requires planning and good timing. It's a long-term strategy. The vampire exit begins as you wrap up your learning experiences. When the dread of fixing up your résumé sets in, implement the vampire exit. It will have a greater impact over the long-term than your résumé, which only functions as a short-term solution.

Before leaving a workplace, seek out people who interest you. Ask them for coffee and a conversation. Simply ask, "I'm really interested in learning about your background. Would you like to grab a coffee this week?" People love to talk about themselves. Learn as much as you can from people without telling them you're leaving.

Then take advantage of any learning opportunities. This sounds counterintuitive. Investing more into the company you're trying to leave feels backward, but it will keep you motivated and engaged at work. Your manager won't guess that you're about to leave. You also might find additional opportunities in your organization. You might find a new position that's a fit for your new skills. It's entirely possible that in a vampire exit you start to suck the organization dry and decide to let it live.

The vampire exit builds a foundation for a future of career changes. Use it every time you need to leave a job.

Create Your Jump Story

It's been drilled into our heads that we must always be networking to succeed in our job search. We've been told this so much that we're tired of it. The anxiety of always being on and always promoting our professional selves is real.

People get connected to jobs in all kinds of ways. In the job search, it is mighty helpful to have someone throw a job your way. You don't have to be at events or promote yourself all the time to get that. You simply need to talk about your job search goals openly. People can't help you unless you tell them what you need.

It's really that simple. You've spent your career transition claiming your space. Now it's time to claim your job search space. Get excited about your next step. When someone you haven't seen in a while asks the usual, "What's been going on?" Tell them you're excited about starting a new career because you've been putting in all the work. Tell them what type of work you're looking for. Ask them to keep an eye out for you for any opportunities that might be a fit. You don't have to ask them for a job. If people like your enthusiasm they'll remember you. Which means they'll look out for you.

Reclaim your narrative

A lot of job seekers stay in jobs because they're worried about what they'll tell a future employer. But here's the truth: you create your own narrative. You don't have to tell your future employer anything you don't want to. Leave complicated situations out of your jump story. You don't have to share details about why you left a previous job. It's actually quite common to gloss over the unimpressive parts of your professional history.

In MBA programs, I coached people on the many ways to spin your prior experience. Did you leave a job because you were doing two jobs and not getting paid enough? You left because there was no opportunity for advancement. Did you work in a job where your boss made people cry? Then you left because there was no opportunity to develop your skills further.

These aren't lies. If you work in an environment where you aren't being paid well for the amount of work, you probably don't want to advance. Think of your story as a translation. Just as companies translate their company culture into smiling About Us pages on the company website, you translate your experience into a shiny message.

Do not feel bad for this. The reality is that you shouldn't have to tell a company why you left your previous job. The reason you left has no reflection on your character or ability to do the job. Companies only ask you this because they have the power.

Let's put an end to all the secrecy around job seeking. Reclaim your power by creating an engaging, positive narrative about your future success. Create a jump story that tells the world what you want. Don't hide the fact that you're searching. Don't get so paranoid that your boss might find out that you avoid telling people you're looking for something better. Instead, create your jump story and get ready to share it with everyone who will listen. Celebrate what you've learned and where you're headed. You never know where it might lead.

EXERCISE: Create Your Jump Story

One of the hardest parts of being a career-changer is trying to fit who you were with what you're doing now. Building a jump story helps you create a narrative that explains your career transition. A jump story is the answer to the questions Why did you change? and WTF do you want now? As a career-changer, you've got one hell of a story. You've made a big change. You've learned and explored. A good jump story communicates your motivations, interests, and curiosity. It's a nice little package that you give to people so they understand your professional self.

Some people call it an elevator pitch. But elevator pitches are static. They assume you'll always tell the same story. Jump stories are flexible. You adapt your jump story to the context of your discussion. If you're catching up with an old friend, you might tell them about your journey and what type of job you want now. If you're talking to an employer, you'll need to give them a story about why you changed careers and how it prepared you for the job you want.

Start by reflecting on what you've done already in your career transition. Think about what you want next. Answer these questions:

- Why did you change careers?
- What have you learned in your learning experience?
- What type of work interests you?
- Why does this type of work interest you?
- What type of company are you interested in working for?
- What subjects or ideas are you curious about?

Use the answers to the questions to shape your story. A jump story is a quick summary. Once you have a narrative, prepare to tell it in under 30 seconds. People's attention spans are short. Here's an example of my jump story:

> *I've had quite a nontraditional career. I've worked in roles that connected me to people—whether I was managing global programs, selling adventure travel, or career coaching students. I decided to change careers so I could build my technical skills. I'm obsessed with artificial intelligence and how it's implemented in the workplace. I want to work for a company that is hyper focused on reducing bias in algorithm design.*

Tell your jump story to people you meet. Adapt it as you go. It's meant to shift and change. Define yourself on your own terms.

The Robots Will Hire You Now

The job search is changing in ways that your parents won't recognize. Companies are increasingly adopting technology that uses artificial intelligence and machine learning to automate the hiring process.

From résumé screening by AI to interview chatbots to predictive analytics that determine who's most likely to leave a job, the list of startups transforming the hiring process is long. In 2017, over half of Human Resources technology investments went to companies offering products and services powered by artificial intelligence. Many of these new technologies go beyond screening applications with a traditional résumé and cover letter. Many use external data, such as public social media posts, combined with machine learning to evaluate or predict if you're a fit for a job inside their organization.

Entelo is an intelligent recruiting platform used by companies like Target, PayPal, and Wayfair. It uses machine learning to determine whether a candidate is a fit for an organization. Its algorithm searches the interwebs to find publicly available data about you. In Entelo's own words, their technology provides "in-depth insights into each prospective candidate by surfacing key data points not found on the traditional résumé, like a candidate's career highlights and progression, company fit, their likelihood of switching jobs soon, and the details yielding to their unique market value."[56]

Recently, the *Wall Street Journal* profiled a company called Frrole that built an AI platform that builds a behavioral profile for every job seeker. The company creates a behavioral profile

---

[56]Entelo, "Candidate Insights."

based on social data taken from publicly available data from sites like Twitter, GitHub, and LinkedIn. They also take into account your social influence scores. Their website promises the ability to rank and analyze candidates using just an email address.

After they capture your online data, they analyze it to determine where you fit into the big five personality traits: Extroversion, Agreeableness, Conscientiousness, Neuroticism, and Openness to Experience. All of your data is then given a score for Learning Ability, Stability Potential, Attitude and Outlook, Action Orientedness, Need for Autonomy, Teamwork Skills, and General Behavior. The final score is your role fit score. You appear in a ranked list of other candidates with a score based on whatever public data the algorithm has found about you.

The future of hiring is much more than a recruiter looking at your Facebook picture. It's a world where algorithms are searching for your publicly available data and analyzing it to determine your hireability. It's a world where companies like HireVue, a video interview platform, use an algorithm to evaluate a candidate's video responses using 25,000 data points including facial microexpressions and tone of voice.

All these companies claim to apply scientific methods to their process and reduce bias. Like most emerging AI companies, there isn't a method for verifying their claims independently. We're forced to take their word for it.

We are in a brave new world of hiring. As job seekers, we are not in control of this process, but we can start asking curious questions to push for transparency. If you encounter companies that use automated tools to make hiring decisions, ask curious questions:

- What technology do you use to evaluate candidates?
- How do your algorithms score candidates?

- How do candidates rank if they don't have online profiles or publicly available data for algorithms to find?
- How much weight do hiring managers give their AI recommendations and scoring in the hiring process?

Take control of your online data

With algorithms scouring the internet for your data, you need to take control of your digital footprint. Most of us have at least a decade's worth of posts, likes, comments, and more online. Do you know everything that you've put out into the world? Do you know what others have put out into the world about you? It's a scary proposition, thinking our online interactions can be used to evaluate our ability to do a job. But it's happening. You need to be prepared for it.

Start by Googling your name. Go beyond the first results. Go deep. What are people writing about you? Have you written posts that are no longer relevant to your life? Check your social media feeds. What shows up? Are your social media privacy settings on lock?

If you see things that don't paint you in a positive light, work on getting rid of them. There are a few ways to work on this. Either ask Google to update their cache, ask the webmaster directly to remove it, or work with a reputation management firm. Change your social media handles. Create fake accounts for friends, real accounts for professionals. Delete old tweets or any other public posts.

Cleaning up your Google search results is only half the story. If human resources is going to use software to analyze your public data, then create professional data to find. Bring your professional self into the online space. LinkedIn profiles are a must, but there's more to do to shape your digital footprint.

Start by leaving a trail of sizable crumbs of your professional life online by creating and distributing small pieces of professional content. Build a GitHub profile to show employers you can code. Put your design concepts on Dribble to show your creativity. Launch a YouTube channel or upload a SlideShare presentation to show you understand how you communicate with audiences. Share articles on Twitter related to the industry you're targeting. Create a blog or start a micro podcast to talk about areas of professional interest.

You can also create a personal website that showcases your work and professional interests. Curating an online professional presence lets you show your ideas and expertise. A personal website will get a hiring manager's attention. According to a company called Workfolio, 56 percent of hiring managers are most impressed by personal websites.[57] Yet only 7 percent of applicants have one. Not only does a personal website allow you to control your digital profile, it gives you the space to shape your career transition story. It shows you are creative and that you are willing to do more than the average candidate. It shows you can communicate. And, most importantly, it shows your work.

Create a space on your personal website that captures all the projects you work on. Keep all your content positive. Focus on showing off your curiosity, creativity, and ideas.

You don't have to do all of these things, of course. But taking care of your digital footprint ensures that you control the information that algorithms find about you online. Even if we

---

[57]Forbes, "Personal Website."

can't know how algorithms are evaluating us as candidates, we can control what they find. Taking control of your digital footprint also helps you learn valuable skills like digital communication, visual design, and writing for the web—all skills that employers value.

PART FOUR

Living Your Fabulously New Professional Life

CHAPTER 9

Keep Up Your Career Momentum

A Toast to the New You

Hey, new you. You're looking good. How's it feel to be starting fresh? Probably pretty damn fabulous. Let's keep this train rolling. Now that you have a job, it's time to kick some ass.

Punch doubt in the face

The first month in my job as an MBA career coach at Yale School of Management I felt out of my league. I had zero brands on my résumé, no Ivy League background, and definitely no MBA. I was responsible for helping people negotiate salaries for $120,000 at top companies. I was making the most money I'd ever made at that time—$82,000. Yet I felt like an idiot, bumbling through it all. Thanks to help from my experienced colleagues and patience from students, I learned how to do it. By the end of my role,

I was teaching executives from around the world how to become thought leaders.

I felt that same dumb feeling four and a half years later when I walked into an AI startup in San Francisco to be a new conversation designer for their chatbot. I'm not an engineer. I'm 10 years older than the founder and a liberal arts major who loves people and the messiness of qualitative data. I spent the first month of that job terrified they'd realize I didn't have a strong enough technical background to work there. A year later, I've conquered the doubt. Now I partner with AI engineers who use my qualitative analysis and user research to improve how the chatbot interacts with users.

Jumping into a new career is filled with doubt. That doubt is imposter syndrome and it's fierce as hell. It takes over your brain, causing you to forget all the reasons you were hired in the first place. It invites all your insecurities over for a beer and a watch party. Together they watch you fumble through the process of learning and starting over. Imposter syndrome taunts you with shouts like, "Why don't you know this!" and "Why did they hire you?" and "They'll find out you're a fraud eventually!" Sometimes imposter syndrome makes you sweat, other times it causes you to overanalyze everything you say or do.

Imposter syndrome is normal for anyone starting over in a new career. Accept it. And then let's punch it in its stupid face. Visualize it. Each time doubt shows up, punch it in the face. Add some colorful words to your punch if it suits you. You can't let doubt hold you back from better opportunities.

Then reframe imposter syndrome as your brain reminding you that you're brand new and ready to learn. At the start of a new career you're not expected to know it all. You're a tenderfoot. The word *tenderfoot* is a synonym for novice, but it was also used to describe a new person in the American frontier. The frontier was a harsh place for newcomers. They had to adapt quickly. I love the word because we all feel a bit tender when we start anew.

Tenderfoot also implies a temporary status. At the start of every new career adventure you're a tenderfoot. But step by awkward step, you build knowledge and apply it in new contexts in your new career. Once you get the hang of things, you grow out of tenderfoot status, ready to claim a new space. Before you know it, you're an old hand at things.

Imposter syndrome will hit you throughout your career change. This cycle of tenderfoot to old hand status repeats with each career change. Whether it's learning a new skill or starting your new job, you're going to battle it. That's okay. When you feel imposter syndrome, remember to punch doubt in the face.

Build a career strategy with the 2×2 method

Now that you've done the hard work of changing careers, start thinking about future you. Get the most out of your current role by following the 2×2 method. The 2×2 method is your commitment to reflection, learning, and skill building throughout your new position. It's designed to keep you agile. You don't have to know what your next step is in order to follow the 2×2 method.

The 2×2 method is simple. Each time you start a new job, commit to two years in the role. In those two years, master two skills. Pick one skill that you're good at and want to get even better at. Then pick a Power Skill that you're not as good at and get better at it. At the end of the two years, check in with your professional self. Ask yourself the hard questions: Am I getting what I need in this job? Does the organization I work for support me? Am I valued, financially and emotionally? Have I communicated my achievements and needs to management?

You don't have to change at two years, but you do have to check in. If you feel you're not getting what you want out of the role, change your situation. You've already changed once. It's easy to change again. You might not need to make a career change, but you might need to change managers, teams, or roles. You've already jumped big. Now you can make smaller jumps to get what you need.

If, at the two-year mark, you're still feeling your job, good for you. Restart the 2×2. Find two more skills you want to improve.

Investigate your place of work

Once you've settled into your new job, start exploring your organization. Similar to what you did in the career transition process, investigate the hell out of the place.

An agile employee understands how other departments work. They're curious about other aspects of the organization. They want to understand how everything fits together. Seeking out opportunities to collaborate outside of your team makes you a better employee. According to Harvard Business Review, "Employees who can reach outside their silos to find colleagues with complementary expertise learn more, sell more, and gain skills faster."[58] Make yourself stand out as a motivated employee by getting to know other departments in your organization.

---

[58]Harvard Business Review, "Cross Silo Leadership."

Commit to curious conversations with people inside your place of work who work on projects that are completely different than your own. Seek out people who aren't like you and listen to their perspectives.

The future of work is shaped by people who can work across silos. It's easy to stay put in your department, only working on what matters to you. Challenge yourself to get to know what's going on beyond your scope of work. It'll make you a more agile employee and open up future opportunities for you.

Keep a shit list

Employees frequently make the mistake of assuming their boss knows all about what they're up to. When it comes to promotion time, they assume their manager has kept track of their achievements. In fact, most managers haven't. They're likely too busy with their own world of meetings, budgets, and managing that one grumpy coworker.

As you settle into your new career, keep track of your work. Note the wins and collect positive feedback. When it's time to ask for a raise, you'll have a nice tidy package of accomplishments to show your boss. It'll keep you organized and help you build a narrative that shows how hard you're killing it in your new job.

The easiest way to do this is to keep a shit list. The Shit My Boss Never Notices list is a documentation of your work. This is a list of all the shit your boss doesn't notice. Contrary to the name of this list, everything good goes on the shit list.

It's a living document that you keep on your computer, phone, or notebook. It's living because you add to it regularly. It shouldn't collect dust because you're so busy killing it in your new job. Each time you do something out of the ordinary or get positive feedback on your work, note it. Get an email from a coworker telling you how much they appreciated you? Note it, with the date, and put it in a special email folder. Take on a new project that's outside of your job description? Add it to the list. Learn a new skill or take a class to help you do better in your job? Write that down.

Give back to your power squad

During your career transition, you built a squad of people who helped you on the path to your new career. You immersed yourself in new communities. Now it's time to give back. Check in with people who helped guide you during your transition. See if they need help. Talk to people. Teach something. Your power squad will evolve as you evolve in your career. Keep connected to the people who you admire and who are doing work you're interested in. Share information, check in with their professional goals, and contribute to efforts to build professional communities.

The future is yours to shape

In 2018, the Henn-na Hotel in Japan replaced their robots with humans. You read that right. Humans replaced robots. According to The Verge, the hotel "laid off half its 243 robots after they created more problems than they could solve."[59]

It seems the robots weren't such a great decision, after all.

---

[59]The Verge, "Robot Hotel."

With so much change in the workplace, it's important to remember that the future of work is not set in stone. The headlines may scream about robots taking our jobs, but nothing is guaranteed.

As an agile worker, you have the power to shape the future of work. As you shape your career, find ways to make positive impact and design a workplace that works for all types of humans. Advocate for flexible hours and better wages. Raise up perspectives and people from underrepresented communities. Push back on attempts to make us less human or pay us less for our hard work. Support organizations that support workers. Collect skills and job-hop your way into a leadership role so you can raise your voice in the new world of work.

The future of work is yours to define.

Conclusion

Fifteen years ago, I quit a corporate job that I hated and sold adventure travel to university students in New Zealand. The sales job didn't pay much but it covered my travel expenses. I didn't know what I wanted to do with my life at that time. Few people know the answer to that question at 24. All I knew was that someone was going to pay me to travel and talk to people. That was all I wanted out of a career at that time of my life.

I spent that job traveling all over New Zealand, speaking to audiences of up to 500 students, and hitting my weekly sales numbers. I also hiked glaciers, kayaked in the sea, watched rugby players in stadiums full of rugby fanatics like me, flirted with people with hot accents, and ate more lamb than I ever thought possible. To this day, it is still one of my favorite jobs.

I didn't know how my career would turn out when I took that job. If you had told me then that 15 years later I'd end up writing a book about careers and making chatbots sound more human, I'd have laughed at you. Even though I didn't know what I wanted, I still collected skills. To this day, my super power is engaging audiences because I spent months finessing my public speaking skills in university auditoriums throughout New Zealand.

My ability to engage international audiences with ease was one of the skills I leaned on to get a job at Yale.

From adventure sales to administrative assistant to travel writer to professional career coach and beyond, my career path has been anything but traditional. I didn't know it at the time, but my experience as a professional job-hopper has provided me with a valuable perspective and ability to help others shape their career, adapt to a changing workplace, and embrace a nontraditional career path.

Our career experiences don't follow a neat line. They ebb and flow, shaped by our curiosity and life experiences. The trick to managing the flow is to take control of it. There are no career change gods to swoop in and show you the way. You have to find your own path.

Career changes are an act of professional reinvention and rebellion. They are full of vulnerability. The first step isn't figuring out what you want to do for the rest of your life. It's claiming your space. So, claim yours. Then use the career change formula to shape your path.

**Professional interests + New skills +
Domain knowledge = New career**

Give yourself permission to explore all the career possibilities. Talk to people about their career journeys. Choose a learning experience that fits your professional goals and your lifestyle. Use DIY learning to acquire the new domain knowledge that helps you speak the vocabulary used in your new career path. Don't hide from the job search. Embrace the awkward. Commit to upskilling regularly.

Our careers are much different from the careers of our parents' generation. Companies are changing how they do business, which means they're changing the type of employee they need to succeed. In some cases, that employee is now a robot or automated software. In other, more hopeful cases, it's an agile employee who can work across traditional company silos, learning and applying new skills as they progress in their roles. Our new world of work demands that we change our thinking about career and career progress. The ones who succeed in this workforce transition will adapt, not react.

The future of work is not set in stone. We have more freedom than previous generations did to define how we'll work. We decide when to change careers, when to learn new skills, and what we want from our employers.

You now have the tools to make a career change, and not just this one, but every career change in the future. There's power in that.

It's time to start the process. Claim your space and create your own adventurous career path.

Online Learning Resources for Upskilling

The last decade has seen a proliferation of online learning opportunities. Below are the online learning opportunities covered in Chapter 7.

Online Learning Platforms

These platforms often partner with universities to develop and offer online degree programs.

- Coursera: www.coursera.org
- edX: www.edx.org

Online Tech Programs Focused on Building Digital Skills

These companies offer short-term online programs that teach users digital skills.

- Skillcrush: www.skillcrush.com
- Treehouse Learning: teamtreehouse.com
- Udacity: www.udacity

Online Marketplace for Skills

These websites offer thousands of videos and short courses to learn specific skills. Some are free while others require a subscription.

- Udemy: www.udemy.com
- Skillshare: www.skillshare.com
- LinkedIn Learning: www.linkedin.com/learning

Bootcamps

Bootcamps offer immersive on-campus and online learning experience. The bootcamps here offer online learning options:

- General Assembly: https://generalassemb.ly
- Lambda School: https://lambdaschool.com
- Thinkful: https://www.thinkful.com

Bootcamp Ranking and Review Sites

The quality of bootcamp programs varies greatly. The two web-sites below consistently rank and review bootcamps. Use them to evaluate which bootcamp is a fit for you.

- Course Report: www.coursereport.com
- SwitchUp: www.switchup.org

References

Chapter 1: Reinvent Your Professional Self

1. "Career | Definition of career in English by Oxford Dictionaries." *Oxford Dictionaries.* Accessed 30 May 2019. https://www.lexico.com/en/definition/career
2. "Catch the wave: The 21st century career." Deloitte Insights. Accessed 11 May 2019. https://www2.deloitte.com/insights/us/en/deloitte-review/issue-21/changing-nature-of-careers-in-21st-century.html
3. "Career ladder." Wikipedia. Accessed 30 May 2019. https://en.wikipedia.org/wiki/Career_ladder
4. "Are We Ready For A Workforce That is 50% Freelance?" Forbes. Accessed 19 Apr 2019. https://www.forbes.com/sites/elainepofeldt/2017/10/17/are-we-ready-for-a-workforce-that-is-50-freelance/
5. Ibid.

6. "For Millennials, Is Job-Hopping Inevitable?" Gallup. Accessed 20 July 2019. https://news.gallup.com/business-journal/197234/millennials-job-hopping-inevitable.aspx

7. "When to switch jobs to get the biggest salary increase." Quartz. Accessed 20 June 2019. https://qz.com/666915/when-to-switch-jobs-to-get-the-biggest-salary-increase/

8. "Cutting 'Old Heads' at IBM." ProPublica. Accessed 30 May 2019. https://features.propublica.org/ibm/ibm-age-discrimination-american-workers/

9. "The Hidden Automation Agenda of the Davos Elite." *New York Times.* Accessed 30 May 2019. https://www.nytimes.com/2019/01/25/technology/automation-davos-world-economic-forum.html

10. "BuzzFeed announces layoffs, missed revenue targets." Chicago Business Journal. Accessed 30 May 2019. https://www.bizjournals.com/chicago/bizwomen/news/latest-news/2017/11/buzzfeed-announces-layoffs-missed-revenue-targets.html

11. "BuzzFeed is laying off about 20 people—and hiring 45 more—in another reorganization." Vox. Accessed 30 May 2019. https://www.vox.com/2018/6/7/17439368/buzzfeed-layoff-hiring-reorganization-facebook-business-jonah-peretti

12. "LinkedIn founder Reid Hoffman on the biggest lie employers tell employees." Vox. Accessed 13 May 2019. https://www.vox.com/2015/5/22/8639717/reid-hoffman-the-alliance

Chapter 2: The Future of Work Has Arrived

13. "What jobs will still be around in 20 years?" *The Guardian* (US). Accessed 19 Apr 2019. https://www.theguardian.com/

us-news/2017/jun/26/jobs-future-automation-robots-skills-creative-health

14. "Our Mission." World Economic Forum. Accessed 19 Apr 2019. https://www.weforum.org/about/world-economic-forum.

15. "The Fourth Industrial Revolution, by Klaus Schwab." World Economic Forum. Accessed 19 Apr 2019. https://www.weforum.org/about/the-fourth-industrial-revolution-by-klaus-schwab

16. "Fourth Industrial Revolution brings promise and peril for humanity." *The Guardian* (US). Accessed 19 Apr 2019. https://www.theguardian.com/business/economics-blog/2016/jan/24/4th-industrial-revolution-brings-promise-and-peril-for-humanity-technology-davos

17. "Robots May Take More Than 5 Million Jobs by 2020." Inc. Accessed 19 Apr 2019. https://www.inc.com/fiscal-times/robots-may-take-more-than-5-million-jobs-by-2020.html

18. "Study: Robots to nab 5.1 million jobs by 2020." *USA Today*. Accessed 19 Apr 2019. https://www.usatoday.com/story/college/2016/01/26/study-robots-to-nab-51-million-jobs-by-2020/37411231/

19. "Terminator, Robocop and Atlas the Robot. For workers the plot is grim." *The Guardian* (US). Accessed 19 Apr 2019. https://www.theguardian.com/commentisfree/2016/feb/25/terminator-robocop-and-atlas-the-robot-for-workers-the-plot-is-grim

20. "The Future of Jobs." World Economic Forum. Accessed 19 Apr 2019. http://reports.weforum.org/future-of-jobs-2016/

21. "About." The Pudding. Accessed 30 May 2019. https://pudding.cool/about

22. "6 key findings on how Americans see the rise of automation." Pew Research Center. Accessed 19 Apr 2019. https://www.

pewresearch.org/fact-tank/2017/10/04/6-key-findings-on-how-americans-see-the-rise-of-automation/

23. "Americans Upbeat on Artificial Intelligence, but Still Wary." Gallup. Accessed 19 Apr 2019. https://news.gallup.com/poll/226502/americans-upbeat-artificial-intelligence-wary.aspx

24. "Amazon's Clever Machines Are Moving From the Warehouse to Headquarters." Bloomberg. Accessed 19 Apr 2019. https://www.bloomberg.com/news/articles/2018-06-13/amazon-s-clever-machines-are-moving-from-the-warehouse-to-headquarters

25. "Accenture Debuts Platform That Automated 40,000 Roles." Bloomberg. Accessed 19 Apr 2019. https://www.bloomberg.com/news/articles/2019-01-29/accenture-debuts-platform-that-automated-40-000-roles

26. "Catch the wave: The 21st century career." Deloitte Insights. Accessed 19 Apr 2019. https://www2.deloitte.com/insights/us/en/deloitte-review/issue-21/changing-nature-of-careers-in-21st-century.html

27. "High-Skilled White-Collar Work? Machines Can Do That, Too" *New York Times*. Accessed 19 Apr 2019. https://www.nytimes.com/2018/07/07/business/economy/algorithm-fashion-jobs.html

28. "Artificial Intelligence Hiring Expands Beyond Tech Sector" Burning Glass Technologies. Accessed 19 Apr 2019. https://www.burning-glass.com/blog/artificial-intelligence-hiring-expands-beyond-tech-sector/

29. "Big banks have dire predictions for those who spend all day 'keyboard hitting.'" MarketWatch. Accessed 19 Apr 2019. https://www.marketwatch.com/story/big-banks-have-

dire-predictions-for-workers-who-spend-all-day-keyboard-hitting-2018-06-12

30. "Aminatou Sow's Work Diary: It's Not a Dirty Word. I Want to Be Rich!" *New York Times*. Accessed 19 Apr 2019. https://www.nytimes.com/2018/11/29/business/aminatou-sow-work-diary.html

31. "Curiosity." NASA. Accessed 31 May 2019. https://www.nasa.gov/mission_pages/msl/essay-20090527.html

Chapter 3: The Upskill Revolution

32. "Alexa, why does a baby boomer who doesn't read emails, won't update their browser version and can't rotate a PDF make triple my salary?" Twitter user @tony_charm 23 Jul 2018. Accessed 31 May 2019. https://twitter.com/tony_charm/status/1021593000521162752

33. "How will automation affect jobs, skills, and wages?" McKinsey & Company. Accessed 19 Apr 2019. https://www.mckinsey.com/featured-insights/future-of-work/how-will-automation-affect-jobs-skills-and-wages

34. "The Hard Part of Computer Science? Getting Into Class." *New York Times*. Accessed 19 Apr 2019. https://www.nytimes.com/2019/01/24/technology/computer-science-courses-college.html

35. "Lunch with the FT: Susan Wojcicki." Financial Times. Accessed 31 May 2019. https://www.ft.com/content/e9a378b2-0c5d-11e6-9456-444ab5211a2f

Chapter 4: Imagination Station

36. "A Brief History of 'Choose Your Own Adventure.'" Mental Floss. Accessed 18 Apr2019. http://mentalfloss.com/article/56160/brief-history-choose-your-own-adventure

37. Ibid.

Chapter 6: Exploring

38. "Leonardo's To-Do List: Krulwich Wonders." NPR. Accessed 13 May 2019. https://www.npr.org/sections/krulwich/2011/11/18/142467882/leonardos-to-do-list

39. "Mona Lisa…Da Vinci and the Renaissance." PBS. Accessed 31 May 2019. https://www.pbs.org/treasuresoftheworld/mona_lisa/mlevel_2/mlevel2_renaissance.html

40. "Careers at Glitch." Glitch. Accessed 31 May 2019. https://glitch.com/about/careers/

41. "Places we don't want to go: Sherry Turkle at TED2012." TED Blog. Accessed 2 Jun 2019. https://blog.ted.com/places-we-dont-want-to-go-sherry-turkle-at-ted2012/

42. "Sherry Turkle." MIT. Accessed 31 May 2019. https://www.mit.edu/~sturkle/

Chapter 7: Learning

43. "Some People Learn to Code in Their 60s, 70s or 80s." *New York Times.* Accessed 22 Apr 2019. https://www.nytimes.com/2017/09/22/your-money/some-people-learn-to-code-in-their-60s-70s-or-80s.html

44. "Recovery: Job Growth and Education Requirements Through 2020." Georgetown University: Center on Education and the Workforce. Accessed 14 May 2019. https://cew.georgetown.edu/cew-reports/recovery-job-growth-and-education-requirements-through-2020/

45. "The Bad First Job's Lingering Impact." Inside Higher Ed. Accessed 23 Apr 2019. https://www.insidehighered.com/news/2018/05/23/college-graduates-whose-first-job-doesnt-require-bachelors-degree-often-stay

46. "The Break Into Tech Blueprint: Learn All the Skills You Need To Land the Job." Skillcrush. Accessed 1 Jun 2019. https://skillcrush.com/break-into-tech-blueprintt

47. "Computer Information Systems." Portland Community College. Accessed 14 May 2019. https://www.pcc.edu/programs/computer-info/cyber-security.html

48. "Micro Electromechanical Systems (MEMS) One-Year Certificate." Lorain Community College. Accessed 1 Jun 2019. https://www.lorainccc.edu/engineering/mechatronics/micro-electromechanical-systems-mems-one-year-certificate/

49. "User Experience Design Track." Lambda School. Accessed 1 Jun 2019. https://lambdaschool.com/courses/ux/

50. "SESP Offers New Higher Education Certificate." Northwestern: School of Education and Social Policy. Accessed 23 Apr 2019. https://www.sesp.northwestern.edu/news-center/news/2016/02/higher-education-certificate-program.html

51. "The Narrow Ladder: The Value of Industry Certifications in the Job Market." Burning Glass Technologies Accessed 23 Apr 2019. https://www.burning-glass.com/research-project/certifications/

52. "Time Flies: U.S. Adults Now Spend Nearly Half a Day Interacting with Media." Nielsen. Accessed 14 May 2019. https://www.nielsen.com/us/en/insights/news/2018/time-flies-us-adults-now-spend-nearly-half-a-day-interacting-with-media.print.html

Chapter 8: Searching

53. "Indeed.com Survey: Here's Why People Don't Share Your Job Openings on Social Media." ERE Recruiting Intelligence. Accessed 23 Apr 2019. https://www.ere.net/social-recruiting-behavior/

54. "Meta-analysis of field experiments shows no change in racial discrimination in hiring over time." Proceeding of the National Academy of Sciences (PNAS). Accessed 26 Apr 2019. https://www.pnas.org/content/early/2017/09/11/1706255114

55. "Let's Keep Legal Protections for Older Employees Strong." AARP. Accessed 26 Apr 2019. https://www.aarp.org/politics-society/advocacy/info-2018/keep-fighting-age-discrimination.html

56. "Candidate Insights." Entelo. Accessed 1 Jun 2019. http://www.entelo.com/wp-content/uploads/2018/04/Candidate_Insights_DS0427.pdf

57. "Why Every Job Seeker Should Have a Personal Website, And What It Should Include." Forbes. Accessed 14 May 2019. https://www.forbes.com/sites/jacquelynsmith/2013/04/26/why-every-job-seeker-should-have-a-personal-website-and-what-it-should-include/

Chapter 9: Keep up your career momentum

58. " Cross-Silo Leadership." Harvard Business Review. Accessed 20 July 2019. https://hbr.org/2019/05/cross-silo-leadership
59. "Japan's robot hotel lays off half the robots after they created more work for humans." The Verge. Accessed 26 Apr 2019. https://www.theverge.com/2019/1/15/18184198/japans-robot-hotel-lay-off-work-for-humans

Learn More

Podcast

50 Conversations with Career-Changers

In 2019, I launched a mini-podcast to explore all the different paths to career changes. With curiosity as my driver, I asked 50 people about their career changes. I captured their stories, encouragement, and advice in the podcast *50 Conversations*. Listening to their stories brings this book to life. Their words will give you the motivation to make your next career change, and each one after that.

To listen to the podcasts, visit www.50conversations.com.

Stay Up to Date

The world of work is changing fast. Get beyond the job-stealing-robot headlines with thoughtful insights about the future of work and career changes. Stay up to date on emerging careers, join the debate about robots and our jobs, and explore our changing workplace with *Beat the Robots* newsletter.

Sign up for the newsletter at www.nicollemerrill.com.

Hire Nicolle—Speaking and Training

I'm from a family of magicians, so I was born to woo audiences. I believe career workshops shouldn't put people to sleep. Whether your organization needs soft skills training for technical teams, perspective-shifting talks for executives, or a keynote on the future of work for career-changers, I have a style that engages audiences and motivates them to act.

My speaking experience crosses continents and audiences. My talks have taken me from the US to Canada, Ireland, Denmark, and New Zealand. I've worked with audiences of many sizes and cultures. From global executive training at Yale School of Management to soft skills workshops for data scientists at the annual Machine Learning 4 All Conference to global career training at Cornell Tech to emceeing for digital influencers at the Women in Travel Summit, my custom career talks resonate across audiences and organizations.

For speaking and custom workshop inquiries, visit www.nicollemerrill.com/speaking.

Acknowledgments

Writing is hard. Putting a book together is a whole other level of hard. So, I have many thanks to give. First thanks go to Publish Your Purpose Press for having a full team of fabulously talented people to teach me and guide me through this process. Thanks to Sarina for shaping the awkward first draft and helping me figure out what to do with my adventure stories.

Many thanks go to my mom for encouraging me for years to write a book. She also gets an extra round of thanks for teaching me how to be a communicator and for years of ruthless résumé and cover letter edits that helped me land jobs. Thanks also to my sister for her remarkable timing and encouragement.

The biggest thanks of all goes out to my wife for being so ridiculously funny and supportive throughout this process. She's the best cheerleader and snack maker a writer could ask for.

Lastly, thanks to every single person who has shared their career stories with me. Your stories helped shape this book and I am grateful to have heard them.

About the Author

Nicolle Merrill specializes in emerging careers and professional reinvention. As a liberal arts graduate, she's pursued an adventurous nontraditional career. A four-time career-changer, Nicolle's professional experience has spanned industries and roles. She's written for Four Seasons and National Geographic private jet tours, taught digital communication skills to global executives at Yale School of Management, and sold adventure travel programs in New Zealand. Nicolle was the Associate Director of Career Services at Yale School of Management, where she coached hundreds of professionals through career changes. She currently freelances as a conversation designer and analyst at an artificial intelligence startup. Nicolle's human-centered approach to career changes and relentless curiosity about emerging career trends has led to speaking engagements across the US, as well as in Canada and Ireland.